SUP FOODS
FOR
SUPER YOU

101 foods for improved health and energy

AMBER JESSICA MACKENZIE

With thanks and love to Josh, Rosie and Elroy Mackenzie, Tim Scanlon, Al Gibbings and Kate Cooke.

Special thanks to Norma Flint, for proofreading my books and being a 'super' mother-in-law.

Published by

WP Wilkinson Publishing Pty Ltd
ACN 006 042 173
Level 4, 2 Collins Street
Melbourne, Vic 3000

Tel: 03 9654 5446 www.wilkinsonpublishing.com.au
Copyright © Amber Jessica Mackenzie 2010
Illustrations Copyright © Liz Craig 2010

National Library of Australia Cataloguing-in-Publication entry:

Author:	Mackenzie, Amber Jessica.
Title:	Super foods for super you : 101 foods for improved health and energy / Amber Jessica Mackenzie.
ISBN:	9781921667619 (pbk.)
Subjects:	Nutrition.
	Nutrition--Requirements.
	Cookery--Health aspects.
	Cookery (Natural foods)

Dewey Number: 613.2

Design and layout: Jo Hunt
Printed by Trojan Press

Contents

Symbols used in this book

(!) Warning

(1) Suitable for children over one year of age

(5) Suitable for babies over five years of age

(❁) Phytochemicals

(♥) Nutrients

(☽) Other beneficial Properties

(☺) Feel good food

(✓) Recommended for vegetarians

(✗) Not recommended for children

Introduction

Let your food be your medicine and your medicine be your food
Hippocrates, c.400 BC

Australia is in the midst of an obesity epidemic and nutrition crisis, with up to one third of health problems caused by lifestyle related health conditions. Inactivity and poor nutritional choices are causing chronic health conditions to become prevalent, with the risk of cancer, arthrosclerosis, diabetes and stroke being exacerbated by long-term nutrition choices. These conditions and others are reducing the lifespan and mobility of Australia's aging population.

People make food choices for vastly different reasons: habit, culture, tradition or heritage, weight and body image, economy and convenience, emotional comfort and health benefits. Whatever the reasons are, these choices have a long-term effect on our health and wellbeing. Our health is affected by the wisdom of our dietary choices over the course of our lives. Many people could live longer more active lives if they ate super foods and increased their physical activity.

What is a Super Food?

Super foods are nutrient dense foods that provide health benefits beyond basic nutritional needs. They are also known as 'functional foods'. Eating whole foods (in their complete and unprocessed state) provides a wider variety of nutrients and additional health benefits including preventing disease, extending your life span and creating a better quality of life. In some cases they may even reverse the effects of ageing.

There is evidence to show that some foods contain a greater cross-section of nutrient essentials than other foods. These foods can also contain non-essential nutrients known as antioxidants and phytochemicals. For instance, lettuce is very good for you, but there is a nutritional difference within the lettuce family.

- The recommended daily intake of folate for women (19-30) is around 400 micrograms (mcg). One cup of iceberg lettuce provides about 16mcg of folate, while romaine lettuce contains 64mcg of folate.
- The recommended daily intake of vitamin A for men over the age of 14 is 900mcg. One cup of iceberg lettuce provides about 9mcg of vitamin A, whereas an equal quantity of romaine provides 163mcg of vitamin A.

When it comes to these two lettuces, the romaine contains more phytochemicals and other beneficial properties than the iceberg and in some cases it has double or even triple the amounts. As you can see from this example, there is a big difference in nutritional value just within the lettuce species. However the nutritional content can also be affected by growing conditions and the quality of the seeds. This is where the name 'Super Food' is useful. It provides a label for foods that studies have shown have a higher percentage of nutrients than other foods of the same quantity.

What determines a super food can also be an individual choice. For instance a vegetarian, pregnant woman, elderly person or teenager all have different nutritional needs which will benefit them during growth spurts, recuperation or the onset of degenerative diseases.

Why Eat Super Foods?

Increasing fruit consumption by one serve a day per person would result in direct health care savings of $8.6 million a year for breast and lung cancer alone.
Shane Landon, 'The Apple Report', 2008

Eating a handful of Goji Berries is not going to instantly make you a healthy person, because it is essential that we eat a wide range of coloured foods from a variety of food groups every day, to maintain good health and wellbeing. Having said this, there are some foods that can be especially beneficial during times of illness or age related symptoms. For instance, Zinc and vitamin C can help reduce the duration and intensity of a cold and the probiotics in natural yoghurt help to restore natural gut bacteria after taking a course of antibiotics. These are some of the obvious beneficial affects of food on our health, but what about things like antioxidants and phytochemicals?

What are Antioxidants?

Antioxidants neutralise free radicals by donating one of their own electrons, thus ending the chain reaction. When they lose electrons, antioxidants do not become free radicals because they are stable in either form.
Rolfes, 'Understanding Normal and Clinical Nutrition', 2006

There are hundreds of different molecules, known as antioxidants, some of these are essential nutrients, such as beta-carotene, vitamin C and E and selenium. However some are non-essential, such as phenolics and flavonoids. Antioxidants occur naturally in the body to combat damage done through a process known as oxidation. Oxidation occurs when free radicals from cigarette smoke, processed foods or the sun's rays build up in the body and cause damage. However the body alone does not provide enough antioxidants to combat this damage so eating plenty of antioxidant rich food will prevent the depletion of the body's natural sources. Most fruits, vegetables and herbs contain antioxidants, some of which are useful at combating certain diseases.

What are Phytochemicals?

Phytochemicals are part of a class of non-essential plant nutrients that have a biological affect on the body. They are not vitamins or minerals, but other compounds used by plants to protect themselves against harmful weather and pest invasion. Phytochemicals also have protective and disease preventative qualities for humans. There are over a thousand phytochemicals, some of these include carotenoids, flavonoids, coumarins, ubiquinol, chlorophyll and tannins.

Not a lot is known about phytochemicals but the research is rapidly expanding. What is known is that no single phytochemical can protect against any one disease. It is a complex process that occurs through association with other nutrients, non-nutrients and fibre within the body. The best approach is through a balanced, whole food diet, which includes five to nine serves of fruit and vegetables a day, including herbs and spices.

What is being discovered is that like vitamins and minerals, phytochemicals have different properties; some have antioxidant properties, others imitate human hormonal action and can reduce the symptoms of menopause. Still others stimulate enzymes that could help prevent the onset of breast cancer. For example

- Capsaicin, a phytochemical found in chilli, can help protect DNA from carcinogens.
- Allisin, a phytochemical found in garlic, has antibacterial properties.
- Proanthocyanidins, found in cranberries, helps to reduce the symptoms or risk of urinary tract infection.
- Organosulfur compounds, found in the Allium family of plants (garlic, chives, onions and leeks) have anti carcinogenic properties.

101 SUPER FOODS

1. Acai Berry

Other Names: *Euterpe oleracea*, magic berry and Acai Palm

Fun Facts: Acai are palm trees that grow 15-30 metres tall in hot, wet, fertile forests and estuaries in the Amazon rainforest.

Super Food Facts: This dark purple fruit has one of the highest concentrations of antioxidants of any fruit. In particular it contains anthocyanins, which are the same antioxidant that give red wine its health benefits. Acai is also high in protein, fibre, omega-6 fatty acids and omega-9 fatty acids. The fruit is great for stamina, contains essential amino acids and has anti-inflammatory properties, all which make it a super food for athletes, growing bodies, vegetarians and vegans.

Acai berries are harvested and then snap frozen either in their whole form or as a juice to preserve their super food qualities. Their nutritional content breaks down very quickly during transport and this is one of the reasons Acai is so expensive to buy. A good alternative would be to eat Kakadu plums, blueberries or Goji berries.

Gardening Tip: Acai can be grown in tropical areas of Australia, such as North Queensland. They grow best in a well-drained soil and need regular watering and plenty of mulch and manure.

2. Alfalfa

Other names: *Medicago sativa* and lucerne

Fun Facts: Alfalfa is a herb whose uses predate recorded history. The Romans used the flowers and leaves around 490 BCE and charred seeds have been uncovered in southwest Iran that date back 6000 years.

Super Food Facts: Alfalfa is very good for relieving fluid retention and the symptoms of arthritis as well as cleansing the blood. It is an excellent source of vitamins and minerals including A, C, K and E and is high in protein (amino acids).

❗ People who suffer from Lupus should avoid sprouts as they may trigger an allergic reaction.

Gardening Tips: To sprout alfalfa seeds place a tablespoon in a glass and fill with water. Cover with a piece of gauze using an elastic band to secure it in place. Next day let the water rinse out through the gauze and refill with fresh water. This time rinse it out immediately. Every day for ten days 'water' your alfalfa seeds in this way and watch them grow and grow!

Not only is Alfalfa a super food for your body, but it is also beneficial in the garden. This is mainly because alfalfa has a twenty to thirty foot root system that can draw nutrients from deep within the soil. For this reason it makes a very good rotation crop for depleted soils. It also makes excellent summer garden mulch being both water retaining and full of nitrogen.

3. Almond

Other Names: *Prunus dulcis*

Fun Facts: Almond oil was used throughout history to anoint kings and priests. It has been used for centuries as a skin moisturiser and is very good at slowing the formation of wrinkles. It also makes excellent massage oil and hair conditioner.

Super Food Facts: Almonds are a super food, particularly for vegetarians as they are a useful source of protein and are a good source of thiamine and niacin. They are also an excellent source of Vitamin E and are high in monounsaturated fats. They can help lower blood pressure when used to replace saturated fat in the diet. Zinc, magnesium, potassium, phytochemicals and selenium, all make almonds a nutritional powerhouse.

Almond butter, dark chocolate covered almonds, ground almonds, almond meal (flour) and roasted almonds are just a few of the many ways almonds can be cooked and eaten. Almond meal is gluten-free and makes excellent flour that is ideal for gluten intolerant people. Many recipes can be converted to use almond flour, such as cakes and breads. Another great Almond product is LSA, which is a combination of linseeds, sunflower seeds and almonds minced together. What a super food combination! LSA can be sprinkled on cereal, pasta, pizzas and just about any meal you can think of.

⚠️ Nuts can cause an allergic reaction in some people. If there is a family history of nut allergies or you have any reason to feel concerned, see your doctor.

Gardening Tip: An almond tree makes a beautiful addition to any garden. Not only are they a super food, but they have the most beautiful blossoms. There are also many different varieties, including dwarf varieties for small backyards.

4. Aloe Vera

Other Names: *Aloe barbadensis* and medicinal aloe

Fun Facts: Throughout history the aloe plant has been used for many purposes including a cooling tonic, demulcent, purgative, to counteract the poison from an arrow wound, to expel worms and as a treatment for ulcerated genitals.

Super Food Facts: There is a very long list of beneficial properties that make the aloe plant one of the most important plants to have in your garden. Two of the main benefits are the aloe's ability to heal and soothe burns externally including frostbite, sunburn, dermatitis and radiation burns caused by cancer treatment. The other major benefit is internally, as a treatment for chronic constipation. This is due to the organic compound known as anthraquinone. It is also very good for people suffering from irritable bowel syndrome (IBS) and Crohn's disease.

Ingesting aloe has been a common practice for hundreds of years. In India fermenting the aloe's gel makes a wine called kumaryasava and its juice can be used to treat people with poor appetite or poor liver function.

(!) Avoid aloe vera during pregnancy as the same part of the plant that is useful as a natural laxative can stimulate contractions. High doses can induce vomiting.

Gardening Tip: Aloe vera grows best in a well-drained, slightly sandy soil with a little slow release fertiliser in it. They can be grown indoors, near a sunny window.

5. Amaranth

Other Names: *Amaranthus cruentus*, red amaranth and prince's feather

Fun Facts: Amaranth has a long and colourful history, including being used by the Aztecs in their human sacrifice ceremonies. A combination of amaranth, honey and human blood was mixed together and eaten. The Spanish Conquistadors were so appalled by this practice that they banned amaranth.

Super Food Facts: Recently amaranth has made a comeback as a super food. This is because it is nutrient dense and retains many of these nutrients during processing. Amaranth leaves are high in protein and fibre and the seeds contain a wide variety of vitamins and minerals including potassium, phosphorus and antioxidant vitamins A, C and E.

Amaranth can be used in a similar way to other grains. It can be popped, ground into a thickening agent or flour, sprouted or added whole to soups and other meals.

Gardening Tip: Plant amaranth during the warmer seasons. Seeds are ready when they fall after the plant is shaken.

6. Apple

Other Names: *Malus domestica*

Fun Facts: The Wild Apple is the original ancestor of all 2000 varieties of the apples we eat and grow today.

Super Food Facts: The old saying, 'an apple a day keeps the doctor away', has been used to describe the humble apple's health appeal for many years. Recently studies have discovered even more reason to eat an apple a day. They contain very strong antioxidants activity; inhibit cancer cell proliferation, decrease lipid oxidation and lower cholesterol. Fruits with the highest amount of antioxidants include blueberries, strawberries, Kakadu plums and, at the top of the list, apples. Phenolics, flavonoids and quercetin are three phytochemicals that are responsible for the apple's potent antioxidant and anti-cancer activity.

In and just under the skin is where apples contain the highest amount of nutrients. They can be stewed whole and mixed with banana or avocado to make the perfect baby food. Apples are one of the best and most convenient snack foods, due to their high soluble fibre content.

Gardening Tip: Apples grow best where the climate is cold as they sweeten to perfection after a frost.

7. Apricots

Other Names: *Prunus armeniaca*

Fun Facts: 4000 years ago the apricot was discovered growing in China where it is generally believed to be their oldest cultivated tree.

Super Food Facts: Apricots are a great source of vitamin C, beta carotene (the plant form of vitamin A) and a good source of fibre, potassium, phosphorus, magnesium and calcium. They are considered a laxative due to their soluble fibre content and are useful when treating gallstones and intestinal worms.

Apricots can be eaten fresh, dried, canned or stewed. Cook for about two hours, equal parts apricots and sugar, with a splash of water and four or five whole kernels to make jam. Add a couple of sliced red chillies and the seeds to make apricot chilli jam.

⚠ Most food companies treat dried apricots with the preservative *sulphur dioxide*. This preservative has been known to cause an allergic reaction in some people. You can buy naturally dried apricots that do not contain chemical preservatives.

Gardening Tip: Similar to almond trees, the apricot tree has beautiful flowers and can be found in many varieties and forms including popular dwarf varieties.

8. Artichokes

Other Names: *Cynar scolymus* and globe artichoke

Fun Facts: Artichokes are a member of the thistle family and are not related to Jerusalem artichokes (which in fact don't come from Jerusalem and are not true artichokes).

Super Food Facts: Artichokes contain antioxidants and are one of the best sources of fruit fibre. They are rich in trace elements such as iron, potassium, calcium and phosphorus, as well as containing cynarin and silymarin, both of which are good for poor liver function conditions and the production of bile. Once considered a rich person's medicine, artichokes are beneficial to people who consume a lot of rich, fatty foods.

The whole artichoke heart can be eaten fried, steamed, boiled, or chopped into dishes or broth. The options are limitless. The leaves can also be used to make a medicinal tea. Artichokes grated or chopped finely into an omelette or Bolognaise sauce are a sneaky way of introducing more fibre and nutrients into your child's diet.

Gardening Tip: These plants prefer a sandy soil, but are grown in a variety of conditions. They may need trimming from time to time and produce little 'pups' of baby artichoke plants around the base. These can be transplanted or given away to friends.

Artichoke

9. Asparagus

Other Names: Green asparagus (*Asparagus officinalis*) and sweet purple asparagus (*Violetto d/Albenga*)

Fun Facts: White asparagus has made its debut on many supermarket shelves, but this designer food is nowhere near as good for you as their green and purple cousins. Burying standard asparagus shoots to prevent sunlight from creating chlorophyll within the stalk heads produces white asparagus.

Super Food facts: Purple and green asparagus are packed full of vitamins and minerals. They are high in vitamins K, C and A, as well as folate and chlorophyll. The fibre in asparagus has a mild laxative effect, and if eaten regularly benefits the gastrointestinal tract and colon. Asparagus contains glutathione, a phytochemical that helps reduce the chances of cancer.

Asparagus is best eaten fresh, within a day or two of buying or picking. It can be made into soup, pureed into a dip, used in omelettes or a frittata, or baked for 10 minutes with butter. Cook purple asparagus briefly to retain its colour and health benefits.

Gardening Tip: New asparagus plants should not be harvested for three years. However, in this time they make an attractive fernlike garden plant. Between 8 to 12 years, asparagus produces regularly and heavily.

10. Avocado

Other Names: Avocado pear, alligator pear, and *Persea americana*

Fun Facts: Technically the avocado is a large berry. Evidence that avocados were around about 10,000 years BCE was found in a cave in Mexico.

Super Food Facts: The avocado is very easily digested and full of antioxidants, vitamins C and E, as well as magnesium and beta-carotene. It is tasty source of vitamin D, which helps builds strong bones.

Avocados are also an excellent source of potassium and contain plenty of monounsaturated fat that has the potential to lower blood cholesterol when combined with a low saturated fat diet.

Avocado makes an excellent weaning food and can be mixed with banana to sweeten it. Avocado can be used to make dips and salads and are great on pizzas or sandwiches.

Gardening Tip: There are many different varieties of avocado and as long as it doesn't get a heavy frost the avocado will endure. Apart from choosing a variety to suit the climate you live in, also be aware that they grow into huge trees and are not suitable for the average Australian backyard. However, if you have a larger block of land then an avocado tree would be a valuable asset in your garden.

11. Banana

Other Names: Sweet banana, dessert banana, *Musa acuminata* and banana palm

Fun Facts: Today's 'yellow' banana is a mutant of the original banana plant that was not sweet and was only used in cooking.

Super Food Facts: Like avocados, bananas are high in potassium and contain magnesium. Both are very good for treating hangovers and dehydration. Bananas are a good source of vitamin C and B6.

Bananas are extremely versatile. They can be baked, blended into smoothies and mashed. When cut and tossed in desiccated coconut they make an excellent side dish to curry. Bananas past their best eating time are ideally used to make banana cake.

Gardening Tip: Bananas aren't trees or palms. They are more like perennial herbs. They like to be clustered in with other plants and to be mulched heavily. Plant them in a fertile, well-drained soil and water regularly.

12. Barbados Cherry ➊✾♡☾

Other Names: *Malpighia glabra*, acerola and West Indian cherry

Fun Facts: The Barbados cherry has a long history as a bonsai plant because of its small leaves. For this reason it is also grown as hedges.

Super Food Facts: Relatively unheard of until around 40 years ago when clinical studies discovered the Barbados cherry's very high concentration of vitamin C. They are also a good source of vitamin A, potassium and folate and are loaded with antioxidants and phytochemicals. However, some super foods are medicinal only in regular, small doses. Health food stores sell the Barbados cherry in capsule, powder, juice and syrup form.

❗ Too many Barbados cherries can cause diarrhoea due to an excess of vitamin C in the body.

Gardening Tip: The Barbados cherry is a tropical to subtropical plant. Young trees do not tolerate frosts very well, but if protected they do become more resistant as they mature. Lightly prune after fruiting.

13. Barley ✾♡☾✓

Other Names: *Hordeum vulgare* and malting barley

Fun Facts: Barley has been commonly used throughout history to make alcoholic beverages and as an animal feed. In more recent times it is used as a health food. Barley comes in many forms to suit its many purposes and has a long history that dates back to being one of the first domesticated crops.

Super Food Facts: Barley has the ability to regulate blood sugar levels for a longer period of time than wholegrain wheat. It contains eight essential amino acids, which are the building blocks of proteins. This makes barley an excellent food for vegetarians and vegans. Barley grass is also a super food, as it is very high in chlorophyll and the antioxidant Superoxide Dismutase (SOD). SOD protects many of the cells exposed to oxygen in the body.

Drinking barley grass has many reputed health benefits, including providing essential and non-essential nutrients and it is a fantastic internal cleanser.

Barley grass can be juiced through most home juicing machines. It can also be bought in a convenient powder that can be added to drinks, soups, stews, breads and sauces.

Gardening Tip: Barley grass can be sprouted from the seed in a tray. They need plenty of sunlight and to be watered daily.

14. Bee Pollen & Royal Jelly

Other Names: N/A

Fun Facts: Bee pollen is collected and made by worker bees from the male seed of flowers. Royal jelly is made from this pollen and fed exclusively to the Queen bee. Queen bees can live up to six years where as the average worker bee lives for only a few weeks.

Beekeepers use a technique where they trap some of the pollen from their bees, but not all of it. This is then either dehydrated or frozen because bee pollen is highly perishable. It is best to obtain bee pollen from the closest supplier possible as this is thought to have further therapeutic benefits such as reducing the chances of an asthma attack.

Super Food Facts: Bee pollen and Royal Jelly contain a powerhouse of vitamins and minerals and are considered a natural vitamin supplement. There are plenty of outlandish claims about them, but the simple truth is that if you require an extra pick-me-up and don't want to take a processed pill, bee pollen or Royal Jelly can help during times of convalescence and in conjunction with a healthy diet.

Bee pollen can be added to smoothies for an extra nutrient kick. Try mango and banana, with yoghurt and bee pollen. Royal Jelly is generally taken in small doses by itself.

(!) Bees and bee products can cause an allergic reaction in some people. See your doctor if there is a family history of allergies or you have any reason to feel concerned.

Gardening Tip: Bee keeping is a fasinating hobbie that is also beneficial to your garden. Bees play an important role in fruit and vegetable production. They pollinate the flowers and increase crop production.

15. Beetroot

Other Names: *Beta vulgaris*, spinach beet and sugar beet

Fun Facts: The bulbs were once only ever used for medicinal purposes, the main ailments being toothaches and headaches.

Super Food Facts: The beetroot bulb is high in fibre, potassium and contains vitamin C. The red colour, *betaine*, has stimulating and cleansing properties. Beetroot also helps with the uptake of oxygen in the body. The green leaves of the beetroot plant are rich in beta carotene, calcium and iron and can be used in salads and cooking in a similar way to spinach. The whole beetroot plant is excellent juiced with apple, carrot and ginger.

Beetroot is naturally sweet and is excellent for young children who are fussy eaters. It is also a very good immune booster. Try baking beetroot or juicing with apples and freeze as icy poles. Grated it can be added to soups, pies, pasta dishes, toasted sandwiches and it makes an excellent moist chocolate cake.

(!) In certain people beetroot can tint the colour of urine bright red. This may look alarming, but is nothing to worry about.

Gardening Tip: Grow from seed in the cooler months, but keep moist as they tend to go woody and are not as sweet if left to dry out for too long. Mulching around the bulbs as they swell also prevents them going woody.

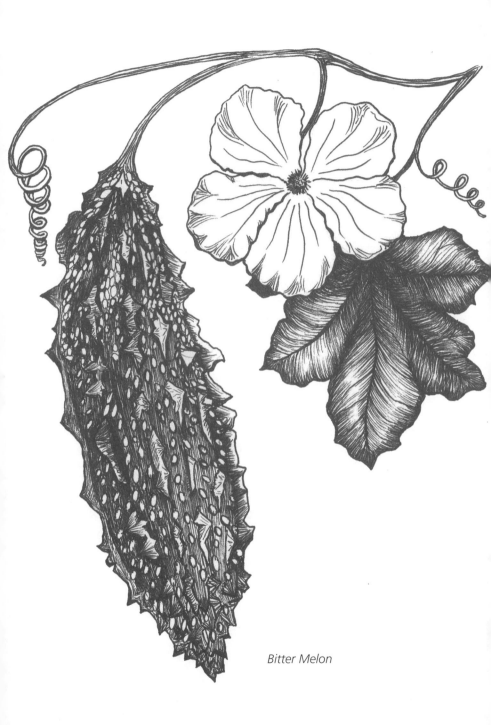

Bitter Melon

16. Bitter Melon

Other Names: Foo-Gwa, balsam Pear, *Momordica charantia* and plant-insulin

Fun Facts: Bitter melons have a long history of use in China as a medicine and food.

Super Food Facts: Bitter melons are very nutritious and come loaded with beta carotene, iron, potassium, phosphorus, fibre, calcium and vitamins A, C, B1 and B3. They are most famous for their use as a treatment for type-2 diabetes as they have been found to contain four compounds that help regulate and fuel metabolism and glucose uptake in the body. They have also been used to treat digestive problems, psoriasis and even cancer.

Bitter melons are very versatile with a taste that mellows and blends well with other flavours. They are suitable for stir-fries, meat dishes (including seafood) and curries.

❗ Bitter melon can irritate stomach ulcers and should be avoided by pregnant women.

Gardening Tip: Plant during the warmer months of the year; hot summers, plenty of water and mulch will produce the best results.

17. Blueberries

Other Names: *Vaccinium spp*

Fun Facts: Blueberries are from the heath family and most of this genus is shrub-like.

Super Food Facts: The colour of blueberries is due to anthocyanin pigments, which are bioflavonoid antioxidants. They are one of the best fruit sources of these antioxidants, which have the ability to neutralise free radicals and prevent disease and premature aging from occurring in the body. They help fight disease by strengthening the immune system and raising haemoglobin and oxygen levels in the blood. This is due to a range of nutrients, in particular vitamins C, E, and A, as well as selenium, copper, zinc and iron.

Where possible eat as a whole fruit because the blueberry skin contains very high concentrations of vitamins and antioxidants. Try blueberries baked, tossed in salads, pureed and dribbled over chocolate ice-cream, frozen, blended into drinks or juiced into power smoothies.

Gardening Tip: Most blueberries grow wild in climates that are cool and have a frost, however there are some cultivated varieties that are suited to warmer regions in Australia. Ask your local nursery what type grows best in your district.

18. Bok Choy

Other Names: Chinese white cabbage and *Brassica rapa chinensis*

Fun Facts: The name *bok choy* comes from the Chinese word meaning *soup spoon*, owing to the curative of its leaves. Bok choy is reputed to have *Yin* properties, which are cooling.

Super Food Facts: Bok choy is a high antioxidant super food loaded with a whole host of other nutritional ingredients – vitamins A, C, B6, beta carotene, calcium, fibre, folic acid, potassium and, depending where it is grown, iron. Baby bok choy is tenderer, but the mature dark green tops are the true super food as they are high in phytochemicals and chlorophyll. Bok choy Is most famously known as an ingredient in wonton soup and stir-fry dishes where it is often added last. The baby leaves are very good in salads.

Gardening Tip: Bok choy grows very easily from seed and will self-sow if left to its own devices. Keeping them well watered ensures the roots continue to shift which prevents them becoming hard and bitter.

19. Broccoli

Other Names: *Brassica oleracea* var. *italica*

Fun Facts: As part of the Brassica family, broccoli is closely related to cabbage and cauliflower. The name *broccoli* comes from the Italian word for arm or branch, owing to the shape of the flower heads – like little trees.

Super Food Facts: Green broccoli is high in chlorophyll, where as the purple variety is rich in antioxidants. Both are high in vitamin C, folic acid, fibre and potassium as well as a load of other beneficial nutrients.

Broccoli keeps very well in the freezer, so if you get a bumper crop, harvest the lot, wash and cut and then freeze immediately in sandwich bags or lidded plastic containers. Stored this way the broccoli will last for weeks and the nutritional value is snap frozen.

Gardening Tip: Not only is broccoli a super food that helps prevent cancer, but it's an attractive garden plant with pretty little flowers. I recommend buying seedlings to start with and then either let the plant self sow or collect the seeds and plant them in a well drained, mulched and manured spot in your garden.

20. Brown Rice

Other Names: *Oryza sativa, Oryza glaberrima* and whole brown rice

Description: Many of the traditional sayings about rice have to do with the high level of work involved in its production. In the Philippines they say, "One grain of rice equals one bead of sweat." These sayings remind and encourage people to appreciate the hard work that has gone into the production of such a simple and popular food. Not only does rice provide half the daily calories for half the world's population, but brown rice in particular is one of the healthiest foods you can eat.

Super Food Facts: Removing the bran and germ layer drastically reduces the nutritional value of rice. Polishing removes the aleurone layer and the essential fats, thereby reducing the health supporting nutrients even further. For instance, on average white rice contains 65% less vitamin B3 and 75% less vitamin B1 than brown rice. 85% of the vitamin B6 content and half the manganese are destroyed converting brown rice to white rice, not to mention the time, money and human resources used in the process.

Brown rice is particularly high in manganese and one cup can provide around 85% of your recommended daily intake. Manganese deficiency includes dizziness, premature loss of hair pigment, skin rash and high blood sugar levels. Brown rice is also a good source of fibre, selenium, thiamine, iron, phosphorus, potassium and folic acid. Brown rice is a super food because it fills you up for longer and provides a wide variety of essential nutrients and antioxidants. This has a two-fold affect; it helps curb food cravings and helps to maintain a healthy weight due to feeling fuller for longer.

Brown rice takes longer to cook than white rice. However it is less likely to break up and go soggy so can be added to soups and stews. Many countries eat rice for breakfast, lunch and dinner.

Gardening Tip: Rice is grown in fields called 'paddy fields' and requires lots of water and humidity.

21. Brussels Sprouts

Other Names: *Brassica oleracea Gemmifera* Group

Fun Facts: Brussels sprouts are probably the most demonised vegetable in the history of food. This is in part due to their pungent smell when cooked, but also, too much of a good thing can create an aversion, particularly in children whose taste buds are more sensitive than adults.

Super Food Facts: Brussels sprouts are high in protein, but are incomplete. This means they do not provide all the essential amino acids. However, when combined with a whole grain they provide all the essential amino acids, which is great news for vegetarians and vegans. They are an excellent source of vitamin K, C, and A. They are also a good source of folate, manganese, fibre, potassium, vitamin B6 and B1, tryptophan, iron and omega 3 fatty acids. The healthiest and tastiest way to eat Brussels sprouts is to steam them and eat with béchamel sauce.

Gardening Tips: Brussels sprouts, as a member of the Brassica family, are closely related to cabbage and broccoli. They grow on long stems, twenty to forty on each. Brussels sprouts grow well in the Australian winter.

22. Burdekin Plum

Other Names: *Pleiogynium timorense*

Fun Facts: You may not be able to buy Australian native fruits fresh from the supermarkets, but there are many condiments available that make use of our native fruits in a way that makes them more palatable. Stars of *The Cook and The Chef*, Maggie Beer and Simon Bryant, as well as Mark Oliver (Australia's leading Aboriginal chef) regularly create recipes that replace imported fruits and meats with locally grown natives. Burdekin plums are very sour but become more palatable a day or two after they have fallen from the tree.

Super Food Facts: The CSIRO has found that Burdekin plums have five times the antioxidants of blueberries, which are renowned for having one of the highest antioxidant content of any fruit.

Gardening Tip: Burdekin plums grow in a variety of habitats in sub-tropical and tropical climates. They can grow up to twenty metres high and the timber is highly sought after by wood turners.

23. Bush Tomato

Other Names: *Solanum centrale*, desert raisin, desert tomato, wild tomatoes and akatjera (Aboriginal name)

Fun Facts: Grown on small silvery bushes with fruit that can be eaten fresh or dried and rolled into a paste. Dried bush tomatoes are often bottled in olive oil and eaten in a similar way to olives. Aboriginals rolled the dried paste into bricks for storage.

Super Food Facts: Like many Australian native foods, the bush tomato is attracting much attention and not just because it is versatile to cook with. Bush tomatoes are full of potassium and calcium and a great source of antioxidants and phytochemicals.

❗ There are some species in the 'Bush Tomato' family that are poisonous. They can look very similar to an untrained eye.

Gardening Tip: The Bush Tomato grows in the dry, desert region of central Australia. They prefer a sandy soil and low humidity. Aboriginals often left them on the bush until they were semi-dried. This gave them a distinct, intense flavour that is stronger than their relative, the garden tomato.

24. Cabbage

Other Names: *Brassica oleracea* var. *capitata*

Fun Facts: In ancient Roman times, burnt cabbage was mixed with lard and used to disinfect wounds.

Super Food Facts: Cabbage is an underestimated and much maligned vegetable, which is very high in many beneficial vitamins and minerals. It is packed with vitamins C and K and is famous for its *indoles* content. Indoles are a compound that, according to recent studies, lowers the risk of some forms of cancer. Cabbage also contains vitamin B6, which is important in the metabolism of energy, and vitamin A, which protects and provides skin and eye health. A substance known as S-Methylmethionine found in cabbage is responsible for relieving gastric ulcers, however this substance can cause flatulence. Red cabbage has more vitamin C, phytochemicals and antioxidants than green cabbage.

Sauerkraut or sour cabbage is a fermented German dish made with cabbage. Cabbage is also used to make coleslaw, which is a great dish, particularly if you mix in some apple and walnuts; two other super foods.

Gardening Tip: Cabbages are a winter crop that should never be grown in the same place as a previous crop from the Brassica family (broccoli, cauliflower, Brussels sprouts). Good drainage is essential for a successful cabbage crop. Spraying with pyrethrum, which is a natural insecticide, prevents caterpillars. Always spray after rain and when it's not windy.

25. Capsicum

Other Names: *Capsicum annuum L*

Fun Facts: Capsicums are actually a fruit. There are many colours but the darker ones are the healthiest – with red and purple being the super food in this group. The vitamin A and C content in both of these is much higher than in the green and yellow capsicums, however all capsicums are an excellent source of phytochemical and antioxidants.

Super Food Facts: There are a number of different, but brightly coloured varieties of capsicum, but the main ones are red, yellow, orange and green. All capsicums are super good for you, however the different colours provide relief for a variety of different ailments. In general capsicums are a rich source of vitamin C, beta carotene, bioflavonoids and capsaicin. Capsaicin is used topically in creams that relieve arthritis pain. Capsaicin is also thought to have anti-carcinogenic properties.

Some people are allergic to capsicums. It is often an allergy to the capsicum skin. Roast or grill capsicums until the skin turns black and then peel and remove the seeds. Capsicums make an excellent casing that can be stuffed with vegetables, rice, olives, and anchovies and baked in olive oil.

Gardening Tip: Grow capsicums in the warmer months, in a light friable soil with lots of mulch and well-rotted manure added. If you live in a hot climate, water around the base of the plant and avoid wetting the leaves.

26. Cardamom

Other Names: *Elettaria cardamomum*, cardamun and choti elaichi

Fun Facts: Real cardamom is expensive, second only to saffron, however there are many substitute cardamom products, but Elettaria cardamomum is the true ancient cardamom spice. Malabar and Mysore cardamom are the two Indian varieties. Mysore is the more pungent variety and has more cineol and limonene content. These two compounds are volatile oils. Cineol is also the principle oil found in eucalyptus leaves, and limonene is found in the rind of citrus fruit.

Super Food Facts: There are two main benefits from eating this super spice; the first is as a relief and treatment for laryngitis and bronchitis. This is in part due to the cineol content, and the second is as a digestive tonic. Both cases benefit from cardamom's ability to ease spasms, whether they are in the bronchial tract or in the stomach due to flatulence and cramps. Cardamom is a warm spice that is good at improving blood circulation and in India they believe it balances out the dosha energy groups – Kapha, Vata and Pitta.

Cardamom is used extensively in Indian cooking not only in curries and pulse dishes but also as an ingredient in desserts and drinks, including chai tea. The oil is used as a mouth freshener and is often mixed with other spice oils such as rose, bergamot, clove and orange.

Gardening Tip: Being a plant native to India, where cardamom grows wild in the forests, it likes hot humid weather distinct to that area.

27. Ceylon Spinach

Other Names: *Basella rubra*, Malibar spinach, *Basella alba*, Indian spinach and vine spinach

Fun Facts: This very old and useful plant also comes in a purple variety that has a slightly different nutritional composition, but is also packed full of vitamins and minerals.

Cardamom

Super Food Facts: Ceylon spinach is a super food because it has one of the highest flavonoid contents for a vegetable. It is loaded with vitamins A and C, iron, calcium, magnesium, folate and manganese. Ceylon spinach is a good source of chlorophyll and, depending on the soil quality, can have good amounts of zinc and selenium. This slightly succulent plant is also rich in soluble fibre.

Very similar to English spinach, hence the name. Ceylon spinach can be eaten raw or cooked into pies, stews and casseroles – any recipe that calls for traditional spinach can have Ceylon spinach used in its place.

Gardening Tip: Ceylon spinach grows well in summer when English spinach, which is only a distant relative, goes to seed. Ceylon spinach is a vine that can be grown on a trellis and the flowers can be cut off as soon as they form so that all the energy goes into producing the edible leaves.

28. Chai Tea

Other Names: *Masala chai* and spiced tea

Fun Facts: Chai means 'tea' in Hindi. It has been converted into a slang word for tea in English speaking countries where they say, 'char'. It is over 5000 years old and can be traced directly to the ayurveda system of healing, which today is one of the most influential healing systems in Eastern medicine.

Super Food Facts: The combined beneficial properties of the ingredients in chai tea make it a super drink. The benefits include: antiseptic and analgesic properties (cloves), treats flatulence and acts as an internal antispasmodic (cardamom), calmative and antacid (fennel), blood sugar regulator and anti-microbial (cinnamon), and antioxidant and anti-inflammatory (ginger).

Chai tea has a few variations but is generally thought to combine the sweet and savoury flavours of cardamom (base spice); star anise, cinnamon, cloves, ginger, black tea, honey, peppercorns, milk and fennel. Because Chai tea was traditionally used for its healing properties, the recipe has as many variations as there are ailments it is said to cure. The above is generally accepted as the traditional recipe.

Gardening Tip: Most of the ingredients in chai tea can be grown in your garden. In particular black tea is often grown as an ornamental plant because it has lovely scented little flowers. Being from the camellia family it grows well in a temperate climate, in a well-drained soil. Camellias are self-sufficient once established.

29. Chia Seeds

Other Name: *Salvia hispanica* L. and salba

Fun Facts: Chia seeds contain a smorgasbord of nutrients and were a staple crop of the Mayan, Aztec and Native American people.

Super Food Facts: Chia seeds are a plentiful source of antioxidants, omega-3 fatty acids and omega-6 fatty acids. They are high in calcium, soluble fibre and contain all the essential amino acids, making them a complete protein. The nutritional value of chia seeds makes them an excellent food for vegetarians, vegans, people suffering from depression and Attention Deficit Hyperactive Disorder (ADHD).

Pinole is a flour that has been made with chia seeds. Chia can be used fresh, ground and roasted. It is recommended that you hydrate the chia seeds in water first. They absorb about nine times their volume in water and this creates 'chia gel', which is sometimes mentioned in recipe books. Chia gel can be used as a thickening agent in cakes, pies, desserts and dressings and is tasteless.

Gardening Tip: Chia mainly grows in hot climates with low humidity. Scatter the seeds on top of a turned soil and rake in. They need lots of sunlight and water but avoid wetting the tops of the plant as the seeds are mucilaginous in nature and will quickly turn slimly.

30. Cherries (sour)

Other Names: *Prunus cerasus*, sour cherry, morello cherry and tart cherries

Fun Facts: In the 1800s Korean Buddhist monks made tea with cherries.

Super Food Facts: All varieties of cherry contain disease fighting antioxidants and phytochemicals. However, according to some studies, it's the sour cherry that is the true super food due to its high levels of antioxidants. The morello cherry has very high amounts of beta carotene, vitamin C, potassium, magnesium and fibre. They also contain useful amounts of iron and folate. All cherries contain melatonin, which help to reset the body's internal clock. This makes cherries a very useful and natural remedy for jet lag. To maintain their super food label I would recommend eating cherries fresh or dried as a snack food and avoid sweetened, preserved and dyed maraschino cherries.

Gardening Tips: Sour cherries grow on smaller trees to the sweet cherry and like the sweet cherry do not require a pollinator. They need a cold winter for fruit set and a light prune after harvest.

31. Chilli

Other Names: *Capsicum annuum* and chilli Asian fire

Description: Chillies have been cultivated for 5000 years and have been used for some very unique reasons. In the south of India chilli was believed to have supernatural powers and was used to deter curses and the evil eye. Chillies even have their own God.

Super Food Facts: Like most super foods, chillies are no exception in their high antioxidant content, but you can't eat a handful of chillies in quite the same way as you can blueberries or cherries. Chillies are unique in their own right because not only are they high in vitamins C and A and a good source of vitamin E, but they also contain capsaicin which has been shown to kill cancer cells.

Capsaicin is also proving to provide pain relief when used topically by osteoarthritis patients and to help reduce nerve fibres swelling in people who suffer from migraines. Most of the capsaicin (the stuff that makes chillies hot) is in the seeds and ribs. These can be removed before cooking to tone down the flavour.

Gardening Tip: Chillies are a hardy plant that grows extremely well in our Australian summers. The chilli (fruit) can be left on the bush to dry and then harvested as required or you can pick the lot when ripe and freeze them fresh. We occasionally put a couple through the juicer and add the juice to curries, pasta dishes and chilli con carne.

32. Cinnamon

Other Names: *Cinnamomum zeylanicum*, also known as Ceylon cinnamon is more expensive and often referred to as 'true cinnamon'. *Cinnamomum cassia* is also known as Saigon cinnamon or Chinese cinnamon. It is related to *Cinnamomum zeylanicum* and is used as a cheaper substitute.

Description: Cinnamon is made from the bark of the cinnamon tree. This is dried and rolled into quills and can also be powdered. Cinnamon was part of the embalming ingredients for the ancient Egyptians and has been used extensively in ancient civilisations in beverages and medicines. Mixed with honey, cinnamon was used to treat insect bites (externally) and arthritis (internally mixed with hot water).

Super Food Facts: Cinnamon is popular in Chinese medicine where it is used to treat flatulence, diarrhoea, and menstrual pain. Most of these benefits are due to cinnamonaldehyde, a compound that gives cinnamon its distinct aroma. There is a lot of research being conducted into cinnamonaldehyde's usefulness in treating people with type-2 diabetes. So far the results are positive in that about a teaspoon of cinnamon a day can help lower blood sugar levels. Cinnamon is a very versatile spice. It is used in Moroccan cooking to flavour couscous and in Indian cooking to make curries. The Chinese use it as part of their five-spice mix and to make chai tea.

Gardening Tip: Cinnamon is a tropical plant that requires good rainfall. Similar to Acai berry, it requires a fertile, well-draining soil.

33. Coconut Water

Other Names: *Cocos nucifera* and agua de coco

Description: Coconut water is not the milk of a mature coconut, but a clear liquid that is found in green coconuts. If you don't live on a tropical island where coconuts drop from trees then you can buy coconut water from your local Asian supermarket.

Super Food Facts: Coconut water is not only a thirst quenching drink; it also makes a very good medicinal tonic to treat diarrhoea, fever, fatigue and headaches. This is because it contains saline and albumen, two substances that help balance electrolytes in blood. Coconut water is sterile and is similar to human plasma. For this reason it was injected directly into the bloodstream of soldiers during the first World War, until a suitable blood transfusion arrived. This is unique to coconut water and there are very few things that can be injected into the blood stream with beneficial results.

Coconut water is high in potassium, magnesium, sodium and natural sugars. It is truly nature's energy drink and is readily accepted by the body. It makes an excellent sports or endurance drink. Athletes and pregnant women can use coconut water as an energy drink. Its main culinary use is in a cocktail, mixed with rum (rum, by the way, is not a super food, but taken in moderation may be beneficial to your smile).

Gardening Tip: Coconuts are hard to grow anywhere where the weather falls below 15°C.

34. Crab

Other Names: Blue crab, snow crab and horseshoe crab

Food Facts: Crab fossils date back to the Jurrasic period, making them one of the oldest species on earth. There are around 4, 400 varieties of crab and every region seems to have its own species. Most of these have five pairs of legs, with the front two being larger.

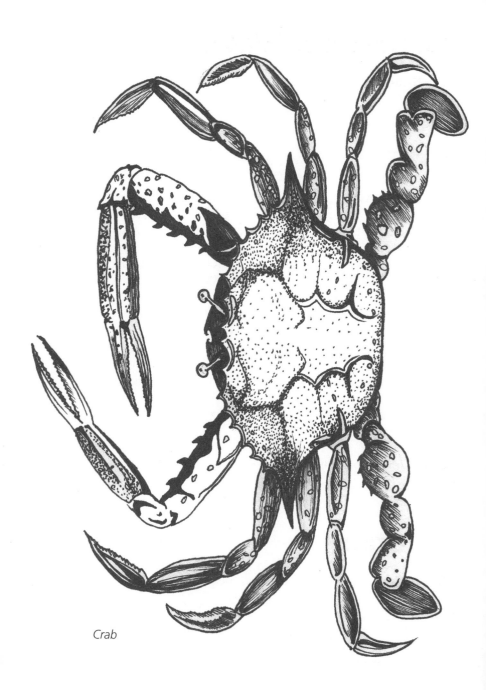

Crab

Super Food Facts: Crab meat is rich in nutrients and low in saturated fat. It is high in protein and omega-3 fatty acids. Omega-3 fatty acids reduce inflammation and are beneficial in helping to reduce the symptoms of premenstrual tension and balance hormonal activity. Omega-3 fatty acids are also gaining a reputation for alleviating depression, arthritis and skin complaints, such as eczema and acne. Crab meat is high in B12, zinc and copper.

Buying Tip: Some varieties of crab (blue crab in particular) are low in mercury. Another tip is to consider where you buy your crab. A sustainable crab fishery is best, this is because some farms clip off and sell crab meat claws, not killing the crabs but cruelly forcing them to regenerate their claws.

Putting a live crab into boiling water is not the best cooking method. It also causes them an enormous amount of stress and this affects the taste of the meat. To kill a crab quickly, lift the flap on the underside to reveal a small hole and jab this quickly with a sharp object.

35. Cranberries

Other Names: *Vaccinium macrocarpon* (large variety) and *Vaccinium oxycoccos* (small variety)

Fun Facts: In 1578, the herbalist Henry Lyte noted the many remarkable healing properties of cranberries. Listed were gout, rheumatism, diarrhoea, constipation, scurvy, fevers, skin infections, eczema and genital infections.

Super Food Facts: Cranberries are getting a lot of attention lately and this has prompted the funding of research into their many health benefits. The most documented benefit is the ability to treat urinary tract infection. This is a condition where the E. Coli bacteria enter the urinary tract. Cranberries contain the antioxidant *proanthocyanidins*, which has a natural antibiotic action and prevents the bacteria from adhering to the lining of the bladder.

Cranberries have many other health applications including helping fight plaque formation, viral infections and regular consumption helps prevent stomach cancer and ulcers. Cranberries are full of quinic acid, which gives them their bitter taste and helps stop kidney stones developing. Cranberry sauce was first commercialised in 1912. Cranberry sauce can be made raw or cooked. Either way it is served cold with turkey. For the best results cranberry juice should be consumed unsweetened.

Gardening Tip: Cranberries grow in cool climates and are a perennial, self-pollinating shrub. They grow up to two metres high and are found growing in bogs and wetlands where miner flooding occurs.

36. Crimini Mushrooms

Other Names: *Agaricus bisporus*, white button mushroom, portabella and pizza mushroom

Fun Facts: Crimini mushrooms are one of three types of white button mushrooms. They are often thought of as a vegetable but are actually a fungus. The mushroom is the fruiting part of the fungus, which contains all the seeds, called spores.

Super Food Facts: Crimini mushrooms are an important addition to the diet, particularly for vegetarians. They are high in selenium, vitamins B2, B5 and B3 as well as copper and potassium. A lot of research has been undertaken about crimini mushrooms with much pointing to this mushroom's ability to reduce the rate of cognitive decline in elderly people and its ability to lower the risk of prostate and breast cancer. This is due to crimini's high levels of selenium, which are thought to help control free radical damage.

One of my favourite crimini recipes is to fry them in olive oil with a nob of butter, thyme, garlic, salt and pepper. I use toasted sourdough bread, but any bread will do. And that's it! Bon appétit!

Gardening Tip: White button mushrooms are the most popular mushrooms grown in Australia. They are readily available in kits and can be grown in a shady, dry area away from vermin and other pests.

37. Dark Chocolate ⑤ ♥ ☽ ☺

Other Names: Bittersweet chocolate

Fun Facts: The alkaloid *theobromine*, which helps produce the feel-good effects of chocolate are toxic to cats and dogs.

Super Food Facts: Dark chocolate is packed full of flavonoids, which as an antioxidant protects against free radical damage. A small amount of dark chocolate a day, combined with a low fat and refined sugar diet can help lower blood pressure and cholesterol levels. Dark chocolate raises serotonin levels and stimulates the production of endorphins, which act as anti-depressants and makes us feel good. The less processed varieties are the healthiest as the cocoa retains more flavonoids. Chilli hot chocolate is a very good after dinner treat, and it combines two super foods.

Gardening Tip: The cocoa tree (*Theobroma cacao*) can be grown in tropical gardens and grows up to twenty metres tall.

38. Dates ① ☽ ♥ ❀

Other Names: *Phoenix dactylifera* and date palm

Fun Facts: The whole tree has proved useful for one thing or another for over 4000 years. The wood is used to build houses, the leaves to make cords, baskets and even furniture, the fruit and seeds in recipes and sauces, and the heart of the tree is even used as a vegetable in some countries.

Super Food Facts: Dried dates have one of the highest concentrations of polyphenols, antioxidants and nutrients of any fruit and are one of the best natural sources of fibre and potassium. Potassium is a nutrient that is not stored in the body but is lost through perspiration. It is essential for muscle contractions and helps to reduce sodium levels. A high sodium level increases a person's risk of stroke and puts additional pressure on the kidneys.

Dates also contain a variety of B vitamins, magnesium (also essential for muscle contractions) and natural sugars, making them a high-energy snack food. Date paste is used in many recipes to produce a thick, sweet sauce. It is often added to milk drinks, cakes and bread mixes.

Gardening Tip: Dates grow on female date palms in tropical weather. After 3 to 5 years the palm can produce an extraordinary amount of fruit up to 30 metres in the air.

39. Eggs

Other Names: Clutch

Fun Facts: Chickens have been domesticated since 600 BCE. Traditionally a French bride would break an egg on her front doorstep for good luck and fertility.

Super Food Facts: One egg contributes significantly to a person's daily vitamin and mineral needs, including vitamins A, B2, B12, D and E and the minerals phosphorus, selenium, iron, iodine and zinc. Eggs contain the best source of lutein and zeaxanthin, two antioxidants that are essential to the proper functioning of the eye. For this reason eggs also help prevent macular degeneration and cataracts of the eye. Eggs can also be a rich source of omega-3 fatty acids, depending on what the chickens are fed. These eggs are often labelled as omega-3 enhanced.

The French have over 685 different ways of cooking an egg, including my favourite – the omelette. Omelettes can be cooked with just about anything, but consider feta cheese, thyme, parsley and cherry tomatoes. That's a fourfold super food!

❗ Eggs can cause an allergic reaction in some people.

Chickens in your Garden: Chickens are very easy to maintain and a pleasure to own. They produce fresh eggs that taste better than any store bought egg you can buy and they will dispose of your kitchen scapes, turning them into a potent manure.

40. English Spinach

Other Names: *Spinacia oleracea*

Fun Facts: Popular folklore has it that spinach is a rich source of iron and calcium, which it is. However, it also contains oxalic acid and this affects the body's ability to absorb the iron and calcium.

Super Food Facts: Spinach is an extremely good source of vitamin K and A, manganese, folate and magnesium. It is also packed with other nutrients such as iron, vitamins C, B2, B6 and E as well as calcium, potassium and dietary fibre and a host of other nutrients in smaller amounts making this a truly super food. Spinach is one of the highest sources of Alpha Lipoic Acid, which is an antioxidant phytochemical that protects against heart attack, cancer, cataracts and helps prevent the onset of cognitive decline. Steaming is the best way to cook spinach as it preserves its natural goodness.

Gardening tip: English spinach is sometimes confused with silverbeet, which grows all year in temperate climates. Silverbeet is a great spinach substitute and the green leaves are equally as good for you and very easy to grow. Both English spinach and silverbeet grow well in winter from seeds planted 2cm under a fertile soil. Because it's the leaves you will be eating and not a fruit, high nitrogen fertiliser such as old cow, sheep or chook manure will produce the best results. Good drainage is essential so if your soil is predominantly clay, add some dolomite first, then dig and water this through.

41. Figs

Other Names: *Ficus carica*

Description: The fig, like the date palm, is an old plant with many uses. In some countries the leaves are used in cooking and have been found to have super food potential as well. Fig leaves may prevent the growth of certain types of cancers and they lower triglycerides levels in the blood stream. The sap of the fig tree irritates human skin, but has been used traditionally to remove warts. The wood is porous and comparable to balsa wood.

Super Food Facts: Figs contain high levels of potassium, calcium, magnesium, iron, copper, manganese and vitamins A and C. Dried figs are an excellent source of calcium and fibre. They are packed full of natural sugar, make a great energy food and are easy to transport.

Figs are a wonderfully versatile food that can be stewed, poached, stuffed, ground, baked or blended. Because it is an ancient food its culinary usefulness is comprehensive.

Gardening Tip: Fig trees have a long life and grow quite large. The fruit needs to be protected with bird netting.

42. Flaxseed

Other Names: *Linum usitatissimum* and linseed

Fun Facts: Flax is another one of those uncommonly useful plants. The flax fibres are used to make linen and are also used in the production of some paper products. Egyptian mummies were wrapped in linen made from flax and the seeds are one of the richest sources of omega-3 fatty acids. There are about 200 species of *linum* plants, including some very beautiful flowering varieties often grown in rockeries and dry gardens as ornamentals.

Super Food Facts: Flaxseeds are a beneficial super food that can alleviate mood swings, inflammation, high cholesterol and stabilise blood sugar levels. Flaxseeds are high in soluble and insoluble fibre, most B vitamins, magnesium, manganese and omega-3 fatty acids. They are a great source of antioxidants and phytochemicals. Because they contain mainly healthy fats and are high in fibre, flaxseeds are an excellent food for people who want to lose or maintain weight. Flaxseeds are often recommended to vegetarians as a great source of omega-3 fatty acids in their diet. Flaxseed and oil are rich in lignans, which help to balance estrogens levels. They can be added to smoothies, cereal and stir-fries. The oil can be taken in capsule form or about a tablespoon a day.

Gardening Tip: The flax plant grows in sunny, well-manured soil. The seeds are harvested when they are 90% brown.

Garlic

43. Garlic

Other Names: *Allium sativum*

Fun Facts: Not only does eating garlic dissuade vampire attacks, but it also keeps many illnesses at bay. It was even thought to be a cure for the Plague. Garlic was carried in ancient Roman times, by soldiers to give them extra courage and luck.

Super Food Facts: Garlic helps strengthen the immune system and can prevent or reduce the duration of a cold. Two components of garlic, diallyl sulphides and allicin, have been proven to have beneficial health effects. Allicin is an antifungal and diallyl sulphide, which is more stable then allicin particularly during cooking, has a positive effect on cholesterol levels and aids in the prevention of heart disease and high blood pressure. This is due in part to diallyl sulphide's ability to thin the blood, thereby reducing the risk of blood clots and stroke.

Garlic can be crushed, roasted, blended and chopped. Medicinally it can also be juiced with other vegetables and fruits to cure a sore throat or cooked with ginger and then added to lemon and honey as a flu remedy.

Garden Tip: Plant the individual garlic bulbs with the paper still on, tip side up. They are a winter plant and sometimes benefit from being chilled in the fridge a week before planting. Because garlic is a small plant many bulbs can be grown close together (about 10cm apart depending on the variety). Once the stems turn brown and dry out they can be harvested and left to cure in a cool dry place. If you leave the stems on garlic can be plaited for easier storage.

44. Ginger

Other Names: *Zingiber officinale*, gan jiang and ginger root

Fun Facts: Ginger is related to cardamom and turmeric and is native to Southern Asia. Queen Elizabeth I popularised the use of ginger in the kitchen by encouraging her cooks to experiment with it. Her cooks are often credited with inventing the original gingerbread man recipe.

Super Food Facts: The therapeutic applications for ginger root dates back to ancient times. Many of its medicinal uses have not changed either. It is still used to aid digestion, nausea, menstrual cramps and relieve cold and flu symptoms. More recently, ginger has also been used to treat migraines, arthritis, blood clots and high cholesterol.

Like garlic, ginger is very beneficial when juiced with vegetables and fruits. Taken this way it is particularly soothing on the throat. Fresh, powdered or pickled, ginger is used in teas, curries, stews, soups, and casseroles and is great in chutney and jam.

Garden Top: Cultivated in tropical regions, the ginger plant grows up to one metre tall. Plant a piece of ginger root, sit back and watch it grow. It's that easy!

45. Grapeseed Oil

Other Names: Grape seed oil and grape oil

Fun Facts: Wine maker Joseph Poporly popularised grapeseed oil after he saw some available in a small shop in Florida in 1998.

Super Food Facts: Grape seeds contain a super oil that is cholesterol free and packed full of omega-6 fatty acids. For these reasons they reduce the bad 'LDL' cholesterol levels and increase the 'good' HDL cholesterol levels. The flavour is mild and it even makes an excellent, non-greasy massage oil.

Grapeseed oil can be used just like other vegetable oil. It is mild flavoured and is particularly useful for sautéing because it has a higher smoke point than olive oil. Smoke point is when oil starts to burn.

Gardening Tip: Grapeseed oil comes from the pulp that is separated when making wine from grapes. Because grape vines are a perennial plant (that is they grow year in year out) choosing a good sunny spot and using proper trellising will put you in good stead for growing grapes in your backyard or orchard. Also don't be shy when pruning a grape – remove about 90% of last year's growth, step back and watch them flourish.

46. Green Tea

Other names: *Camellia sinensis*

Fun Facts: Traditionally black tea, white tea, green tea, oolong and pu-erh tea are all harvested from the same plant, *Camellia sinensis*. But it is green tea that retains the health promoting properties due to the way it is processed. The leaves are steamed and this prevents the polyphenols (which are powerful antioxidants) from oxidising. It's no wonder that the Chinese have been drinking green tea for over 4000 years.

Super Food Facts: Green tea is one of the most researched super foods in modern times. Some of these studies have highlighted the ability of green tea to reduce the risk of oesophageal cancer, reduce 'bad' LDL cholesterol and decrease the development of blood clots (which can lead to heart attacks and strokes). It is also beneficial in preventing tooth decay and halitosis because it destroys plaque-causing bacteria. Green tea can contain as much caffeine as coffee (depending on the brewing time).

While there are many recipes that can have green tea added as a flavour enhancer, it is most beneficial when consumed as a tea as this prevents the oxidation of its health promoting properties.

Gardening Tips: Camellia sinensis can be cultivated in temperate climates and is often grown as an ornamental because of its highly scented flowers.

47. Guava

Other Names: *Psidium guajava*, guayaba and goiaba

Description: Guavas are classified as a berry due to the way they grow in clusters. There are different varieties, including yellow and red cherry guava. Guavas have been used as a traditional medicine to treat colds, constipation, skin infections, scurvy and high blood pressure.

Super Food Facts: Guavas are a great natural source of vitamin C. One guava contains five times more vitamin C than a single orange. They are high in fibre, carotenoids and potassium. Guava has therapeutic qualities that prevent diarrhoea and act as an antibacterial and antibiotic, this is due to astringent compounds in the fruit and leaves. Guavas also have a slight sedative effect.

To get the most nutrients out of your guavas eat them raw or juiced. They are popular in jams and jellies but these are often high in sugar and the cooking time required destroys most of the vitamin C.

Gardening Tip: The guava tree fruits best when it has a pollinator. They should be regularly pruned otherwise they'll grow up to 25 feet tall. Guavas have caused considerable damage as a weed in Fiji, Mexico, South Africa, Hawaii, West Polynesia and parts of Australia. Because of this and to prevent fruit fly damage, they should be netted when fruiting.

48. Hibiscus Tea

Other Names: *Hibiscus sabdariffa*, roselle flor de Jamaica and Hawaiian hibiscus

Fun Facts: The red hibiscus flower is used as a dye for shoes, facial cosmetics and as a tea.

Super Food facts: Hibiscus tea is excellent during times of convalescence as it is high in vitamin C and phytochemicals that contribute to its dark red colour. Hibiscus tea is a diuretic and helps shift salt from the body. It reduces high blood pressure and high cholesterol levels, two of the biggest risks for heart disease.

In Jamaica this deep red tea is made using ginger root, honey, and sometimes rum and is served chilled. To make tea infuse dried flower sepals of the Hibiscus sabdariffa plant in hot water.

Gardening Tip: Hibiscus plants grow well in Australia, particularly where they are in full-sun and protected from cold winds. Good drainage is essential and a light prune every other year is recommended to stop them becoming 'leggy'. Frost damage can see the plants defoliate, but most will bounce back the following year.

49. Kakadu Plum

Other Names: *Terminalia ferdinandiana*, billygoat plum and vitamin C tree

Fun Facts: Kakadu Plum is a deciduous tree, which is unusual for an Australian native. It has large pale leaves and grey, flaky bark. It is a versatile tree used as timber, food and medicine.

Super Food Facts: When compared to blueberries the Kakadu plum (which is more like an almond than a plum) contains five times the antioxidants. This makes it the world's highest fruit source for vitamin C. Kakadu plums contain two phytochemicals that are potent antioxidants - gallic and ellagic acids. Both of these acids have anti-tumour and anti-carcinogenic properties along with a long list of other benefits.

Aboriginals snack on the bitter fruit of this tree. To make it more palatable it can be stewed and made into jams and sauces. It is also popular as a juice, mixed in with other sweeter fruits.

Gardening Tip: The Kakadu plum grows to 10 metres in tropical areas with well-drained soils. The fruit is harvested from March to June.

50. Kale

Other Names: *Brassica oleracea* var. *acephala*

Fun Facts: Kale used to be a very popular vegetable until cabbage exceeded its favour during the Middle Ages. Cabbage (being from the same family) is also very nutritious, but kale's dark green leaves are higher in antioxidant rich phytochemicals and are easier to grow.

Super food Facts: It's not surprising that Kale, another member of the Brassica family, is considered a super food. Kale is exceptionally nutrient-dense and contains very few calories. This makes it an excellent food if you are trying to lose weight. This super food is very high in vitamins K, A and C as well as magnesium and sulphur-containing phytochemicals. Kale has a very broad cross section of vitamins, minerals and other beneficial properties including manganese, fibre, calcium, protein, omega-3 fatty acids, B2, B6, tryptophan and potassium.

There are different varieties of kale and some are quite tough and fibrous. To alleviate this problem the main stem should be removed and the whole plant chopped up before cooking. Kale requires a longer cooking time than spinach and other green vegetables.

Gardening Tip: Kale is grown in the cooler months of the year. It benefits from a light frost, winter sun and well-drained soil. There are also some very pretty ornamental varieties that are pink and purple.

51. Kangaroo Meat

Other Names: Eastern Grey and *Macropus Giganteus*

Fun Facts: Kangaroos have increased in population in Australia to almost plague proportion. This is because of the availability of boar water making them one of the most abundant land animals on earth. Kangaroos are not hard footed like sheep and cattle, which combined with European farming systems have impacted and changed the Australian landscape.

Super Food Facts: Kangaroos are indigenous, relatively inexpensive to cull and one of the healthiest meats you can eat. Not only is it high in protein, iron and zinc, but it is very low in fat, in particular saturated fat. Being a wild animal kangaroo meat is organic and free of hormones and other chemicals. If you like eating red meat this is my number one super-meat recommendation. Use kangaroo meat like any other red meat. Most supermarkets have a variety of cuts, including steaks and sausages.

Gardening Tips: Try kangaroo poo on your garden beds. It's one of the few types of manure you can use fresh and not only is it a slow-release fertiliser but it can sometimes be obtained for free. My family tend to avoid me while I'm out 'collecting', but it's readily available on the mid north coast of Australia where I live.

52. Kombu Seaweed ❶ ❁ ♡ ✔

Other Names: *Laminaria japonica*, konbu, dashima and haidai

Fun Facts: One of the earliest recordings of kombu usage is in a letter dated 797 CE describing it as a gift or tax. However, it was mainly used throughout Asia and was not exported extensively until the 1960s.

Super Food Facts: One of the best super food facts about kombu, a type of edible kelp seaweed, is its very high iodine levels, in fact it is often recommended to people low in this nutrient. Iodine deficiency has become a major concern after it was discovered that low iodine levels in a pregnant woman could affect their child's motor and hearing skills. In fact iodine deficiency is the number one cause of mental retardation in babies. Iodine is needed to make the thyroid hormones and these are essential in regulating growth and energy metabolism. This is a problem in Australia and other countries where iodine is naturally low in the soil. Kombu is used to make a soup called dashi in Japan. It is sold dry, powdered or pickled and can be re-hydrated in water. Kombu is also an excellent source of vitamin K, folate, calcium and magnesium.

Gardening Tip: You can't grow seaweed in your garden but you can use it as a fertiliser. We collect it from our local beach, rinse it, let it dry out in the sun, then walk all over it to crumble it up and sprinkle it around plants.

Limes

53. Lemons & Limes ❶ ♡ ✽ ☾

Other Names: *Citrus limon* (lemon), *Citrus aurantifolia* (lime) and *Eremocitrus* glauca (desert Lime)

Fun Facts: There are many different varieties of lemons and limes and most grow well in warm Mediterranean climates. Three of the most popular lemons are *Eureka*, *Meyer* and *Lisbon*. There is also a native Australian Desert Lime that is smaller and more intense in flavour. Dessert limes have three times the vitamin C of oranges.

Super Food facts: One benefit of consuming lemons and limes is that they are alkalinising to the stomach. Another benefit is that they contain the phytochemical essential oil limonene, vitamins C and B6, potassium and flavonoids. Limonene, like other phytochemicals, is receiving lots of attention due to its ability to detoxify the system and increase enzyme productivity. This is one of the reasons dieticians recommend drinking a glass of water with half a lemon squeezed into it first thing in the morning.

Gardening Tip: Citrus plants like to be fertilised and pruned and the fruit sweetens up in the winter months. There are also some good lemon and lime dwarf varieties that can be grown in pots or even in the garden, and the fruit is full-sized!

54. Lentils ❶ ♡ ☾ ✔

Other Names: *Lens culinaris*, daal, dhal and dal

Fun Facts: Of unknown origin, lentils are widely cultivated and eaten as a staple food or animal feed. Archaeological digs have uncovered lentils around Lake Biel in Switzerland dating back to the Bronze Age.

Super Food Facts: Lentils are a rich source of eight of the nine essential amino acids, making them an excellent source of protein for vegetarians. Mixing them with eggs, nuts, seeds or dairy products will complete the protein chain by adding the missing ingredient, methionine. They also have a good cross-section of other nutrients including vitamins C and A, calcium, phosphorus, folate, fibre and iron. Lentils are a cheap alternative to meat, but should be eaten with vegetables and rice so that the meal contains all the essential amino acids. Of the many health benefits, two are outstanding – lentils help balance blood sugar levels and lower cholesterol levels. Lentils can be stored for an indefinite amount of time. Because of this they need to be rehydrated overnight in cold water or boiled for a more immediate result.

Gardening Tips: Lentils are legumes and grow inside seedpods in the cooler months of the year.

55. Macadamia Nuts

Other Names: *Macadamia integrifolla* (smooth shelled), *Macadamia tetrephlla* (rough shelled), Queensland nut, bauple nut and bush nut

Fun Facts: Even though Macadamias are native to Australia, Hawaii actually grows 95% of the world's crop. They were introduced in 1880 and have thrived in Hawaii's hot, humid weather.

Super Food Facts: Native Australian Macadamias have been given the National Heart Foundation Tick of Approval, mainly due to their high monounsaturated fat content. Macadamias are also high is essential fatty acids which help to balance mood swings and depression. They are also a good source of potassium, calcium, protein, antioxidants and phytochemicals. Fresh or roasted macadamia butter is an excellent way to introduce it into your cooking. As a paste it can be used on toast, in satays, pesto and smoothies.

Garden Tip: Macadamias don't like the frost, but will handle hot summers and cold winters. Also, if you are after a good crop, consider planting two trees, that way they can pollinate each other.

56. Maitake Mushrooms

Other Names: *Grifola frondoso*, hen of the woods and grifolan

Fun Facts: Maitake mushrooms have a history as a medicinal and culinary food. A tea made from these mushrooms was used to strengthen and restore the immune system.

Super Food Facts: Maitake is part of a group of mushrooms considered medicinal. This is because they contain a molecule called 'grifolan' which boosts the immune system and helps prevent cancer cell proliferation. Researchers have found in animal studies that maitake extract can inhibit the growth of stomach and bone cancer and it provides some relief against the side effects of chemotherapy.

Maitake can be used in any recipe that requires mushrooms, but in general when using wild mushrooms less is needed because they are stronger in flavour than commercially grown mushrooms.

Gardening Tip: Maitake mushrooms grow on rotting wood and live symbiotically at the base of chestnut trees.

57. Mangosteen

Other Names: *Garcinia mangostana*

Fun Facts: Mangosteen's health benefits are highly regarded and come not from its white flesh but its deep purple rind. There is a yellow variety of mangosteen (*Atractocarpus fitzalanii*) but it doesn't have the same super food value as the purple variety.

Super Food Facts: Mangosteen has many health benefits. The most reputed are their off-the-chart antioxidant properties and their ability to combat inflammation in the body. Two compounds called Alpha Mangostin and Gamma Mangostin, when isolated and tested were found to have remarkable healing properties within the body. These included having significant anti-inflammatory, antibiotic and antiviral properties. Mangosteen is sold in capsules, but its health benefits are maximised by eating the whole fruit or drinking the fresh fruit drink that is not made from a fruit concentration.

Gardening Tip: These small trees require tropical weather and plenty of moisture to grow.

58. Mulberry

Other Names: Black mulberry (*Morus nigra*), white mulberry (*Morus alba*), red mulberry (*Morus rubra*), morus fruit and the silkworm fruit

Fun Facts: Mulberries are an all-round useful plant. Apart from the health benefits mentioned below derived from the entire tree – the wood is also highly valued and used to make sports equipment: rackets, bats and hockey sticks. Also people feed mulberry leaves to their silk worms.

Super Food Facts: Every part of the mulberry tree has been used medicinally for hundreds of years. In Chinese medicine the leaves of the white mulberry are used to cool the liver channel and to treat colds, fever, headaches and throat infections. The branches and twigs are used to treat rheumatic disorders and upper body pain or illnesses. The bark has a long history as an expectorant and to treat 'hot' conditions and the fruit is a restorative and blood cleanser. Mulberry recipes are mainly desserts such as crumbles, but they can also be used to make jam.

Gardening Tip: Despite the popular nursery rhyme, 'Here we go round the mulberry bush,' the mulberry is in fact a tree.

59. Mustard Greens

Other Names: *Brassica juncea*, mustard plant and green mustard cabbage

Fun Facts: Mustard greens are closely related to kale, another super food and green vegetable often referred to collectively as a "mess o' greens".

Super Food Facts: Mustard greens are among the most nutritious leafy green vegetables you can eat. Mustard greens have a strong taste and are loaded with vitamins A, C, and E, folate, manganese and fibre. They are high in antioxidants and phytochemicals and promote mental function, energy production and cancer protection. They are also an excellent blood cleanser and help balance the acid/alkaline levels in the body. The seeds of mustard greens are used to make Dijon mustard and to make mustard oil. The leaves taste peppery and can be used fresh, steamed or baked. They are not unlike spinach in their versatility and can be mixed with other leafy greens to tone down the strength of their flavour.

Gardening Tip: Mustard greens make an excellent green manure crop between harvest and propagation. They hyper-accumulate heavy metals and are a good plant to use in areas where soils are contaminated. In this case the plants would not be edible for human consumption.

60. Noni Fruit

Other Names: *Morinda citrifolia* and Tahitian noni fruit.

Fun Facts: Noni fruit has been used as a traditional medicine to treat colds and fevers, skin and eye complaints, respiratory and chest infections, as well as a stomach tonic and to relieve colic pain. All parts of the tree are used – even the roots have a traditional application.

Super Food Facts: Many countries don't sell fresh noni fruit, but noni fruit juice is available and while not having the same super food potential as the whole fruit, is still a valuable food source. The University of Hawaii has found a substance they call "noni-ppt" that boosts the immune system and offers

Noni Fruit

protection against some cancers. Noni fruit is eaten raw (despite its bitter taste), cooked or juiced. Some countries use the fruit in a salty curry and Aboriginals roast and eat the seeds.

Gardening Tip: The noni tree is native to Southeast Asia. It grows in a variety of habitats due to its drought resistance and tolerance to different soils including saline.

61. Nutmeg

Other Names: *Myristica fragrans*

Fun Facts: Nutmeg has long been thought of as a super food and cure-all. In China it has been used since the 7th century to treat stomach upsets. However, over-consumption of nutmeg can have a toxic effect on the body. A measured amount of some things makes all the difference between a medicine and a poison.

Super Food Facts: Nutmeg is a super food due to the healing properties of its essential oil. This helps lower blood pressure and is good for treating stomach cramps. Nutmeg is a stimulant and increases brain activity and in small amounts, helps detoxifies the blood.

Often nutmeg is used in sweetly spiced desserts or in smoothies and on custard. The Italians use it to make mortadella sausages and the Scottish haggis is spiced with nutmeg. It is also good sprinkled on Brussels sprouts and in béchamel sauce.

! Large doses can cause palpitations or convulsion.

Gardening Tip: Nutmeg grows in a humid climate but doesn't like to be over-watered. Both a male and female plant is required for flower pollination. Nutmeg is produced from the seed kernel.

62. Oats

Other Names: *Avena sativa*

Fun Facts: Oats is part of a family of grass plants known as *Avena*.

Super Food Facts: Oats contain soluble and insoluble fibre. The soluble fibre reduces the absorption of 'bad' cholesterol LDL. In addition, Tocotrienols, a type of antioxidant found in oats, help lower LDL levels in the bloodstream. Oats help control fluctuating blood sugar levels, conatin phytoestrogen compounds called lignans, which reduce the risk of some cancers, help control blood pressure and hypertension and relieve constipation. Oats are a good source of protein (a major building block of the body) as well as zinc, thiamine, selenium, vitamin E, panthothenic acid and folic acid. Oats can be eaten as porridge with every known berry, nut and seed added, but they can also be used in a bath to relieve dermatitis and dry skin.

Gardening Tip: Oats need to be kept moist until they have germinated. Mulch and fertilise to maintain soil moisture.

63. Okra

Other names: *Abelmoschus esculentus* (and also *Hibiscus esculentus*), gombo and ladies fingers.

Fun Facts: Ground okra seeds have been used as a coffee substitute since the 1800s and were used during World War II when there was a shortage of coffee due to rationing. Okra has also been used to make soap and fibre. Its main use is in soups and is particularly popular in Cajun and Creole cooking.

Super Food facts: Okra is an unusual plant, with a long and sometimes strange history. It's not as commonly used in Australia as other parts of the world, but it should be. It's full of vitamins A and C and also contains iron, folic acid and calcium. It has demulcent and emollient properties and some interesting health benefits due to its fibre content. Okra's fibre binds with toxins and helps to eliminate them from the body. The fibre also helps regulate sugar levels and is an excellent food for maintaining good intestinal bacteria (probiotics). Okra is a valuable plant food but when cooked at high temperatures for long periods of time loses some of its nutritional benefits.

Gardening Tip: Okra grows best in a hot climate where the soil has good drainage, manure and some lime added.

64. Olives & Olive Oil

Other Names: *Olea europaea*. subsp. *europeae*

Fun Facts: Olive trees are one of the oldest cultivated trees and because they live for so long, they are also some of the oldest specimens of tree known to man. Wars have been fought over olive trees, borders defined by them and babies born under them. Olives have seen the whole of modern civilisation and will probably be standing long after we are all gone.

Super Food Facts: Olives and olive oil are a rich source of monounsaturated fats, antioxidants and phytochemicals. Combined with a low saturated and trans-fat diet, olives and olive oil help prevent heart disease, lowers blood cholesterol and the risk of colon cancer. There is a good deal of research to support this statement. The Mediterranean diet has been under scrutiny for years due to its low incidence of heart disease, despite a high fat (predominantly olive oil) diet.

For a healthy, cholesterol lowering bread-spread mix butter 50/50 with virgin olive oil. Olive oil can be used to replace other fats in cooking, and it doesn't lose any of its beneficial qualities.

Gardening Tip: Olive trees like a dry, hot summer and do well in Mediterranean climates. They grow slowly, can live to a ripe old age and don't fully bear fruit until they are between seven and ten years old. However, in the meantime they make an excellent shade tree.

65. Onions

Other Names: *Allium cepa*

Fun Facts: Onions are a durable food source that can be stored in a cool, dry place without spoiling for months. This has made them a very popular food throughout history. The onion's medicinal and cosmetic uses include the prevention of hair loss, to remove freckles, a blood purifier, and cough suppressant.

Super Food Facts: Onions contain sulphur compounds, quercetin and phytonutrients that when cut gives off a distinct odour and eye-watering fumes. These compounds have antifungal, antibacterial, anti-inflammatory and antioxidant properties. For centuries onions have been used to treat colds, infections and breathing problems caused by allergies or asthma. This is not surprising as they are a rich source of vitamins A and C, as well as calcium, potassium, chromium and phosphorus.

Onions are a particularly good food for people suffering from atherosclerosis, arthritis and poor appetite. Red and brown onions are the most nutrient dense and the healthiest types to eat. Today the onion is a favoured ingredient in many recipes all around the world. They are versatile and have enormous health benefits eaten raw or cooked. Onions can be pickled, baked, fried and grilled.

Gardening Tip: Onions are fuss-free to grow. Sow directly into a soil that has had dolomite turned through it. Plant them shallow and keep them well-watered until they are established. Onions grow well in the cooler months of the year.

66. Oysters

Other Names: Sydney rock oysters, Pacific oysters and native oyster

Fun Facts: In Maine, America there is an oyster farm that is one of the most famous examples of a prehistoric trash dump. Once 10 to 15 metres deep with oyster and other seafood shells, it dates back approximately 1500 years.

Super Food facts: In many cultures throughout history, oysters have been considered an aphrodisiac. This is not surprising given that they are one of the richest sources of zinc. Zinc is essential for the production of sperm. Children who have low levels of zinc show a delay in sexual development and puberty. Zinc is also essential for healing infections in the body. Oysters are also packed full of copper, iron, protein, and potassium and contain good amounts of selenium (for healthy hair, skin and nails) and iodine (essential for proper thyroid function).

Oysters can be cooked in many ways: Grilled, marinated, chopped up in pasta, baked on pizza, but I prefer them as fresh as possible with just a squeeze of lemon juice. Mignonette sauce is made with vinegar and shallots and is commonly served with oysters.

Gardening Tip: Oyster shells make a great contribution to any garden. They make a great fertiliser, mixed in with fish bones and water in a lidded bucket. They can also be tossed straight into the garden and are particularly beneficial around fruit trees. Many soils have low zinc levels, so this may help remedy the mineral imbalances within the soil.

67. Papaya

Other Names: *Carica papaya* and pawpaw

Description: Papayas are not trees, despite the fact that they are often referred to as such. They are large-leaved, short lived, herbs with hollow trunks. They grow in tropical climates and do not tolerate frosts at all.

A male and female papaya plant is needed for pollination, although hermaphrodite plants have been found in cultivation.

Super Food Facts: Papayas are rich in proteolytic enzymes that break down protein and aid digestion. This has led to the creation of a powdered papaya supplement that is given to people with digestion problems. It is also used as a meat tenderiser because it literally digests the meat. They are also rich in an antiparasitic compound called carpaine. The seeds are particularly rich in this compound and are a good treatment for intestinal worms. Papaya is a versatile fruit to cook with. If you can't get hold of it fresh then try dried, canned or even the juice. They are all a bountiful source of nutrients, but the only true super food is the whole fruit.

Gardening Tip: Papaya is a fast growing plant that, given the right growing conditions, will fruit for most of the year. Both the ripe and unripe fruit have beneficial properties.

68. Pepita Seeds

Other Names: *Cucurbita pepo* and pumpkin seeds

Fun Facts: The name *pepita* comes from the Mexican-Spanish name *pepita de calabaza*, which means 'little seeds of squash'.
Super Food Facts: Pepita seeds are high in zinc, monounsaturated fat, protein and manganese. They are a good source of magnesium and iron and contain a substance called cucurbitacins that promotes prostate health. Pepitas have anti-inflammatory benefits and help with the symptoms of arthritis. For years pepita seeds have been used as an anthelmintic (an agent that treats intestinal worms) particularly when eaten with ginger and garlic, two other herbal treatments for worms.

Pepita seeds make a great snack, roasted with almonds and sunflower seeds in tamari sauce. They can be added to salads and just about any savoury dish that you can think of. Excessive heat destroys some of the seeds nutritional value, so only roast for short periods of time.

Gardening Tip: Pepitas are pumpkin seeds. If you want to grow pumpkins see super food number 71: Pumpkins.

69. Pomegranate

Other names: *Punica granatum*

Fun Facts: This old and very useful plant has been mentioned in many texts and stories throughout history. Pomegranate flowers and leaves adorn buildings and were depicted in fine needlework on clothes and tapestries. The tree's bark was used to make a yellow dye while the flowers make a red dye. The roots have been used to make quills and the astringent fruit was taken to expel intestinal parasites.

Super Food Facts: Scientific research is backing up anecdotal claims that pomegranates and its juice can help prevent a number of life threatening diseases. In a study conducted using mice it was noted that pomegranates slowed the development of lung and prostate cancers. They also prevented LDL cholesterol from oxidising, which is a leading cause of atherosclerosis. Fresh pomegranate juice thins the blood and helps prevent blood clots forming. Pomegranates are very high in antioxidants, potassium and vitamins C and B5.

Depending on the type of pomegranate they can be sweet or sour. The sour notes come mostly from antioxidant tannins called punicalagins. Pomegranates also contain the antioxidants anthocyanins, which gives them their rich red colouring. In Persia they make a soup out of pomegranate juice. Grenadine is a sugary syrup made from pomegranates that is used traditionally in many recipes and as a cocktail mixer.

Gardening Tip: Pomegranates are grown in sub-tropical to tropical climates. A standard tree grows 4 to 7 metres high but there is a dwarf variety, which is ideal for potting or a small backyard.

70. Porphyra Seaweed

Other names: *Porphyra spp*, nori seaweed and Pacific seaweed

Description: Porphyra seaweed is shredded, pressed and dried in a similar way to making paper. These are then wrapped around rice, vegetables and fish to make nori rolls.

Super Food Facts: Porphyra is very high in iodine, chlorophyll, phycobilins (this is responsible for the distinct red pigment), vitamins A and C, protein and zinc. It also contains mucilage or slime, which comes with its own health promoting properties. Dried porphyra (nori) is higher in vitamin C than oranges and it contains a compound called Taurine which helps prevent gallstone disease. Studies using porphyra have shown it to be effective in reducing stress ulcers. This could be because it contains a substance called porphyran which showed positive results in reducing tumour growth in rats. However, it may also be due to the combination of vitamin C and zinc, both of which are also effective at treating ulcers in the body.

Porphyra seaweed can be bought either dried, powdered, flaked or pressed into sheets. Add it to liquid dishes as with any other green vegetable.

❗ Anyone suffering from hypothyroidism or on a low sodium diet should avoid seaweeds.

Gardening Tip: Seaweed makes an excellent addition to any compost heap or as manure on top of the soil. Porphyra can be rinsed, to remove excess salt and then dried out and crumbled around plants.

Pumpkin

71. Pumpkin

Other Names: *Cucurbita spp*

Description: Pumpkins are from the same family as squash and cucumbers and there are about 27 different varieties. Pumpkin makes an excellent weaning food and rarely causes allergies.

Super Food Facts: Pumpkins are a super vegetable because they are extremely high in beta-carotene, which the body converts into vitamin A. They also contain lutein and zeaxanthin, two antioxidants that are particularly beneficial to eye health and the prevention of cataracts. Vitamin A is an anti-oxidant that helps neutralise free radical damage and is included in many skin care products to help reduce the signs of aging.

Pumpkins contain other nutrients renowned for their anti-aging effects; vitamins E and C, potassium, zinc, fibre and alpha-hydoxy acid. Not only is pumpkin nourishing to the skin but it is an excellent immune booster that helps prevent cell damage. Pumpkin flowers, seeds and meat are all edible. The original pumpkin pie was a pumpkin with the top cut off, filled with spices, honey and milk and baked in a fire pit. The spices were cinnamon, ginger and nutmeg, all wonderfully nutritious super foods.

Gardening Tips: Growing pumpkins is easy! Rogue seeds will germinate and grow like weeds during the warmer seasons. But a little bit of care helps grow more, and bigger, pumpkins. I generally grow them on a raised mound of dirt with plenty of mulch and compost. Smaller varieties of pumpkins (such as butternut) can be trained to grow up a trellis or wired wall.

72. Purple Carrots

Other Names: Purple dragon

Fun Facts: Earliest documentation has purple carrots being used as a medicine – primarily as an aphrodisiac and as part of the ingredients for an antidote to poisoning.

Super Food facts: Orange carrots are an excellent source of vitamin A and contain a whole host of phytochemicals and antioxidants. However, purple carrots are more nutritionally dense than their orange cousins and have twice the amount of beta-carotene and 28 times the amount of anthocyanins. Anthocyanins give food their purple, blue and red colouring. They are a powerful antioxidant that can reduce the risk of some forms of cancer and have anti-inflammatory properties.

A 17th century recipe by Giles Rose (one of the Master Cooks to Charles II, 1682) used purple carrots in a dish called "Pudding of Carrot". This was made with bread crusts, grated carrots, cream, butter, lots of eggs (using mainly the yokes) heaps of sugar, a pinch of salt and the centre of the bread. Basically a bread and butter pudding with purple carrots stewed into the mix.

Gardening Tip: Grown in the cooler months, carrots need to be kept moist for the first two weeks until they have sprouted. Once established they are almost maintenance-free, needing only the occasional weeding and watering.

73. Purslane

Other Names: *Portulaca oleracea*, common purslane, pigweed and little hogweed

Fun Facts: Dr. Artemis P. Simopoulos first brought this succulent plant's omega-3 properties to our attention in 1986. In Greece, where it grows wild and is used in salads and other dishes, purslane is being touted as one of the reasons Greek people have such a low incidence of heart disease.

Super Food Facts: Aside from being an excellent plant source of omega-3 fatty acids, purslane also has one of the highest combinations of vitamins A, C and E of any herb. Purslane is a rich source of glutathione, another antioxidant, and a powerful immune booster. It can also be used externally to treat burns, bites and stings.

Aboriginals used native purslane's poppy-like seeds to make seedcakes. The whole plant can be eaten, including the roots and these are often baked. However, purslane is most commonly used fresh in salads, mixed with natural yoghurt or feta cheese.

Gardening Tip: Purslane has a taproot enabling it to tolerate poor soils and drought.

74. Quince

Other Names: *Cydonia oblonga* and common quince

Fun Facts: Biblical scholars often consider quince the true 'forbidden' fruit in the Garden of Eden. The Portuguese word for Quince is *marmelo*. This is where we get the word marmalade.

Super Food facts: Quinces are high in vitamins C and A, phosphorus, antioxidants potassium and fibre. They are good for lowering blood cholesterol and blood pressure, which reduces the risk of heart disease. Quinces have anti-viral properties and can relieve and suppress the symptoms of gastric ulcers due to their phenolic content.

High in pectin, the quince is most popularly used in jams or marmalade, but they are equally as good poached, stewed or baked. Quince is astringic and not often eaten fresh, but if you can tolerate the taste fresh quince is very good for you.

Gardening Tip: The common quince, like its relatives the pear and apple, does not tolerate humid weather.

75. Quinoa

Other Names: *Chenopodium quinoa*

Fun Facts: Quinoa is often referred to as a grain and is used like one, but it is actually a seed. The name is pronounced *keen-wah*.

Super Food Facts: Quinoa is a super grain that contains all nine essential amino acids and has a protein content comparable to meat. This makes it an excellent food source for vegetarians and vegans. Quinoa is high in magnesium, vitamins B and E, antioxidants, fibre and iron.

Quinoa is useful as an alternative in any recipes that calls for rice. Use like any other grain but be sure to rinse it first. Quinoa can also be used uncooked and ground into flour or used to make sushi rolls (cooked and mixed with tahini).

Gardening Tip: This is a very easy plant to grow in temperate climates. Plant about 30cm apart and harvest when the seeds separate easily from the stalks.

76. Raspberries

Other Names: *Rubus idaeus* (red raspberry) and *Rubus occidentalis* (black raspberry)

Fun Facts: Historically raspberries have practical, medicinal and culinary uses. The juice was used to dye manuscripts and the berries and leaves were used to treat chronic infection, exhaustion and to cure emotional imbalances.

Super Food Facts: Raspberries are very high in vitamin C, folate, potassium, iron, manganese and fibre (due to the seeds). Raspberry leaf tea has been used for its health benefits for years. It is full of tannins and very useful in treating diarrhoea. Raspberry leaves have also been used to tone the uterus in the last trimester of pregnancy. Not only are raspberries packed full of vitamin C, a known antioxidant and anti-carcinogenic, but they contain good amounts of ellagic acids, also well known for their cancer fighting properties. Raspberries spoil easily but can be snap frozen. Cooking a handful of raspberries, a teaspoon of cornflour and some orange zest makes a coulis, in other words a sauce.

Gardening Tip: There are many different varieties of raspberries including a black and purple cultivar. These are equally, if not more of, a super food than the regular raspberry due to their darker colouring. The raspberry is a cool weather-bearing vine that grows best in a loose sandy loam.

77. Red Grapes & Red Wine

Other Names: *Vitis vinifera*

Fun Facts: Grapes are a classic old-world food that have been depicted on temple walls and written about on tablets and manuscripts. They are featured regularly in the bible, including the story of Jesus turning water into wine.

Super Food Facts: Red grapes are as high in antioxidants as blueberries. Like raspberries, red grapes are also a potent source of the antioxidant and anticarcinogen *ellagic acid*. Resveratrol is another anticarcinogen found in red grapes that blocks the development of two of our biggest killers, prostate cancer and leukaemia.

Dried grapes (raisins, sultanas, and currants), grape juice and red wine (in moderation) are all nutrient dense foods. Grape seeds and the leaves are a valuable source of nutrients and can be used in many recipes. From the seeds we get grape seed oil, which is a super food in its own class.

Gardening Tip: Grapes grow well over a balcony that receives plenty of sun. They are susceptible to fungal problems and need to be heavily pruned after they have produced fruit. Water them well while they are fruiting.

78. Reishi Mushroom

Other names: *Ganoderma lucidum*, red reishi and ling zhi

Fun Facts: Reishi mushrooms have a reputation as a heart tonic and are also thought to help with the pain of angina and arrhythmia. They are often referred to as the 'mushroom of immortality'.

Super Food Facts: Eastern medicine says that reishi mushrooms help balance the body and guard against the three major health threats – physical, emotional and energetic. There is plenty of scientific research to back up these thousand year old Taoist claims. Reishi has been shown to have immune-boosting properties that help treat cardiovascular disease, cancer, high blood pressure and infectious diseases. Reishi can replace any mushroom in a recipe. Dried reishi mushrooms make a beneficial tea that is thought to improve blood flow.

Gardening Tip: Mushroom growing kits are becoming more widely available and the varieties that can be grown more diverse. Reishi mushrooms grow on wood chips and the kits can be sourced online or bought from some nurseries.

79. Rocket

Other names: *Eruca sativa L.*, salad rocket and arugula

Fun Facts: Rocket was a very popular herb during the middle ages. The juice was used to treat asthma, coughs and other lung disorders. It fell out of favour until the middle of the 20th century but has now bounced back to become a popular side dish in many restaurants.

Super Food Facts: Rocket has a peppery flavour that is very good at helping to balance the body's acid/alkaline levels. An overly acid body is prone to a host of diseases that over time can become chronic. Unfortunately, today most Westerners have an excess of acid in their bodies. Foods such as rocket, lemon and parsley can help to neutralise this condition and prevent diseases. Rocket is used mainly as a salad green when it is young. As it ages the peppery flavour intensifies. It also makes a great pesto ingredient.

Gardening Tip: Rocket grows from seed in a sunny, well-manured soil. It grows best when it is watered daily as this keeps the roots shifting and stops them bolting to seed.

80. Rockmelon

Other Names: Cantaloupe and muskmelon

Fun Facts: Rockmelons originated from a small Italian village where they were first cultivated over 300 years ago. They are one of the most nutritious melons you can eat. Apart from eating it fresh, rockmelon is a popular dessert ingredient and is often used to make gelato and smoothies.

Super Food Facts: Rockmelon is a great source of vitamins A and C, several of the B vitamins, potassium, folic acid and fibre. Rockmelon has anti-coagulant properties that help prevent blood clots. It also helps replace valuable minerals lost during and after physical activity and the potassium helps prevent muscle cramps.

Gardening Tip: Like pumpkins, rockmelons grow on vines during the warmer months of the year. They do not grow well in humid climates and for this reason it is best to water their root ball and surrounding mulch and to avoid wetting the leaves. This will reduce the chances of the plant getting a fungal disease.

81. Romaine Lettuce ❶ ✤ ♡ ☺

Other Names: *Lactuca sativa L.* var. *longifolia* and cos

Fun Facts: Romaine lettuce is one of the best lettuces for you, but there are other lettuces, particularly the purple and red varieties, that could also pass for super foods. These include Radicchio, red velvet and the reddish-brown types of butternut and oak leaf lettuce.

Super Food Facts: Not all lettuces have the same nutritional value. Different types, particularly the darker varieties, are much more beneficial and nutrient dense. Romaine is one of the most nutritious lettuces you can eat. It includes high levels of vitamins K, A and C, chromium, folate, potassium, lutein and manganese. All lettuces contain chlorophyll and in Chinese medicine are considered cooling (yin). Lettuce is great in salads, sandwiches, soups, or as an edible wrapper.

Gardening Tip: Romaine lettuces grow all year round, unlike some lettuces that can't tolerate the heat. It requires mulching in the summer months and plenty of water to keep the roots shifting, which will prevent them going bitter, hard and bolting to seed. They also self-seed readily and are one of the most fuss-free lettuces to grow.

82. Rosemary & other Herbs ❶ ♡ ✤ ☾ ☺

Other Names: *Rosmarinus officinalis*

Fun Facts: Many herbs are packed-full of flavour and only a small amount is required to season a meal. The long-term benefits of using herbs in meals, tea or topically has been recorded for thousands of years. Among my favourites are parsley, thyme, basil and mint.

Super Food Facts: Rosemary tops my list of super herbs as it has so many culinary and cosmetic health benefits. It can be used to treat depression due

*Rosemary &
other herbs*

to the compound cineole that revives and invigorates the central nervous system. Adding the leaves to a meal helps with indigestion and improves liver function. Applied to the skin and hair, rosemary oil helps strengthen capillaries and has moisturising properties. For this reason it has been used for years as an anti-aging ingredient in cosmetics. The smell of rosemary oil is also good for relieving tension headaches, so mixing a few drops of the oil into your conditioner can have a two-fold effect. It moisturises the hair and invigorates the mind. Traditionally rosemary has been used to season meat but it can make an excellent tea mixed with chamomile and honey.

Gardening Tip: Rosemary grows well from a cutting in a well-drained soil. They do not need much water but require lots of sunlight and as little time in wintry, frosty weather as possible. They are a Mediterranean plant, so dry heat is preferable to humidity.

83. Rye

Other Names: *Secale cereale*

Fun Facts: Historically rye has been dismissed as a poor man's food, but this has no foundation in nutritional science. The aversion to rye may have been due to the susceptibility of the plant to play host to the fungus ergot. Ergot was the original source from which LSD was first isolated. Ergot poisoning causes gangrene, convulsions, hallucinations and even death. People suffering these symptoms were often accused of witchcraft or devil possession.

Super Food Facts: Dark rye, as opposed to light rye is more nutritionally dense than whole wheat. It is high in protein, iron, calcium, zinc and B vitamins. It is also a good source of vitamin E and because it contains both soluble and insoluble fibre, is beneficial for treating Irritable Bowel Syndrome (IBS) and preventing bowel cancer. Rye helps maintain a sense of fullness for longer, in part because it meets our nutritional needs and also because it slows the release of carbohydrates in the body. This is useful if you are trying to lose weight or suffer from type-2 diabetes.

Russia and Poland use rye flour to make bread and there is a traditional Jewish rye bread recipe that uses caraway seeds. These breads are very dark and filling compared to wheat breads. More recently rye has made a comeback as the principle grain used to make some beers.

Gardening Tip: Rye is grown in the winter months for seed or as a mulch crop. Cast the seed on top of a tilled moist soil and press down with the back of a rake or spade. Water well and regularly until the seeds have sprouted.

84. Salmon

Other Names: *Oncorhynchus* (salmon family), pink salmon, Atlantic salmon and cherry salmon

Fun Facts: Historically salmon were considered a part of the ritual passing of the seasons as well as a food source. Life-sized salmon carvings, dating back 20,000 years have been found in a cave called *l'abri du poisson* at Les Eyzies in France.

Super Food Facts: Oily fish such as salmon, mullet, trout and blue-eyed cod are all excellent sources of protein and omega-3 fatty acids. They are also rich in selenium, zinc, vitamins A and D and some B-vitamins. Salmon is particularly good for brain, nerve and cognitive health. The elderly may benefit from eating oily fish as it can help prevent Alzheimer's and Parkinson's disease. Other benefits include skin, hair and nail health, reducing blood pressure and inflammation and it acts as an anti-depressant.

Salmon can be cooked in a variety of ways, the same as with any meat. Wrapped in foil with butter, salt, thyme, garlic and lemon slices and cooked in either the oven or BBQ is one of our family favourites.

Gardening Tip: As with other seafood, salmon bones makes an excellent fish emulsion.

85. Sardines

Other Names: Sardine and pilchard

Fun Facts: Sardines are named after the island Sardinia, in the Mediterranean, where they were once prolific. Pilchard is a term often used interchangeably with sardines. Technically a sardine is classed as measuring under 10cm long and a pilchard as over 10cm long.

Super Food Facts: Sardines, like salmon, are another oily fish that are an excellent source of omega-3 fatty acids. They are like tiny protein energy pills; filled with vitamin D (for stronger bones), CoQ10 (an antioxidant and energy conveyer), B12 (also good for energy production), selenium (for healthy hair, skin and nails) and they have anti-inflammatory properties.

One of the best things about sardines is that they are less likely to have accumulated toxins because of their small size and their low position in the food chain. Canned sardines are a very convenient way to supply the diet with omega-3 fatty acids. If you don't like the smell, try sardines in water or brine, those canned in oil smell strongest.

Gardening Tip: If you used left over sardines to make fish emulsion you would have a very healthy garden. What better way to recycle old food than to use it to grow new super foods?

86. Shiitake Mushroom

Other Names: *Lentinula edodes*

Fun Facts: Mushrooms are more closely related to animals than plants. In fact their closest relative is a unicellular parasite called *Microsporidia*. Shiitake are the world's second most cultivated mushroom.

Super Food Facts: Shiitake mushrooms boost the immune system, help balance blood sugar levels and promote cardiovascular and respiratory health. They contain lentinan, which reduces cholesterol levels, helps ward off viral infections and prevents tumour growth. They are also high in protein all of which makes them an excellent food for vegetarians. Shiitake mushrooms can be bought fresh or dried. Dried mushrooms can be boiled in water and soy sauce to enhance their flavour. This creates a shiitake bouillon (broth).

Gardening Tip: Shiitake literally means 'oak-mushroom' in Japanese, because they grow on the wood of the oak tree. You can buy shiitake kits online that include shiitake spores, which have been impregnated into pieces of dowel.

87. Soybeans

Other Names: *Glycine max*

Fun Facts: Records show that Soybeans have been propagated in China since 3000 BCE. They were used originally as a rotation crop and not as food. During the Chou Dynasty (1134-246 BCE) fermentation processes developed and foods such as miso, tofu, natto and tempeh were created.

Super Food Facts: Soy foods are high in calcium and protein and are one of the most common sources of the phytochemical *isoflavones*, which is a phytoestrogen. Isoflavones are a known preventative of some cancers including breast and prostate cancer, and they can mimic the work of oestrogen. This means that isoflavones act similarly to hormone replacement therapy in helping relieve menopausal symptoms such as hot flushes. Soybeans contain all the essential amino acids, making them a valuable source of protein for vegetarians. They are also high in fibre and low in saturated fats. Soybeans can cause flatulence, but soaking them in water first and then rinsing can remedy this.

⬤ Some people may have an allergic reaction to soy products.

Gardening Tip: Plant seeds in full sun during the warmer months. Soil should be nitrogen rich and kept moist during germination stage. Like most beans they require trellising to support the plants as they grow. Allow the beans to dry naturally on the plant before picking.

Strawberry

88. Spirulina

Other Names: Blue Green Algae

Fun Facts: Spirulina is a tiny micro alga that measures a mere .0196 inches. The Chinese feed it to their chickens and livestock to increase growth and productivity. Spirulina research started in the 1960s. In the 1970s the main area of interest was its nutritional benefits and disease fighting potential.

Super Food Facts: Aside from it being a rich source of protein, spirulina is a potent source of iron, calcium and magnesium, along with vitamins A, C, D, E and a range of B vitamins too. Spirulina can help restore health to people who have been ill, the elderly and anyone who has trouble absorbing nutrients due to bowel disorders such as IBS or Celiac disease. It is a high source of chlorophyll, antioxidants and phytochemicals, but the recommended daily intake should not be exceeded because too much protein can overload the kidneys. Spirulina is sold in powder and capsule form. Poor quality products have been accused of being contaminated with heavy metals; so always buy a product where the source is clearly labelled.

Gardening Tip: Spirulina can be grown under the right conditions. The temperature needs to be above 20°C for growth to occur. It can be grown in a pond or other watertight vessel. Wind and rain encourage growth as they compensate for evaporation and agitate the water, which is recommended so that all the spirulina culture gets equal amounts of sunlight.

89. Strawberries

Other Names: *Fragaria ananassa*

Fun Facts: Traditional folklore used strawberries to cleanse and purify the body, relieve kidney stones, gout, inflamed eyes (using only the juice, no seeds) and to whiten the complexion and remove sunburn.

Super Food Facts: Not only are strawberries a lovely looking fruit, but they are also among the healthiest, with one of the highest levels of vitamin C of any berry or fruit. Vitamin C helps the body absorb iron, so it is important in the diet of vegetarians. Strawberries are a super source of phytochemicals and their bright red colour is due to their high antioxidant levels.

One of my favourite strawberry recipes is called 'Romance in a bowl'. It uses mainly super foods that are thought to also have aphrodisiac properties. As well as strawberries the recipe includes mixed salad greens, carrots, raspberries, walnuts, almond slices, sultanas, feta cheese, seasoned rye bread croutons and an olive oil based salad dressing. Perfect for Valentine's Day.

🛈 Some people may be allergic to strawberries. One of the symptoms includes hives (a rash or skin welts).

Gardening Tip: The best strawberries are home grown ones that are left to mature on the plant. These are often smaller, but are packed full of flavour and are super healthy for you. Growing strawberries is a great way to introduce small children to the joys of growing and picking your own food.

90. Sunflower Seeds

Other Names: *Helianthus annus*

Fun Facts: Sunflower seeds were eaten 5000 years ago and were popular among the American Indians.

Super Food Facts: Sunflower seeds are a rich source of vitamin E, an antioxidant that is not only beneficial to your skin, hair and circulatory system, but helps fight free radical damage too. One of the reasons sunflower seeds are popular with vegetarians and vegans is because they are an excellent source of vegetable protein. They also provide fibre, zinc, selenium, magnesium, iron and potassium. Sunflower seeds can be eaten raw or roasted, hulled or unhulled. Sunflowers make a polyunsaturated oil that is often used to make margarine.

Gardening Tip: Sunflowers are beautiful bird attracting plants that grow on long stems and come in a variety of colours. There are sunflowers that have one enormous flower head and others that are covered in smaller bronze and copper coloured flowers. The seeds from the bigger varieties are easier to harvest and eat and the birds love them!

91. Sweet Potato

Other Names: *Ipomoea batatas* and kumera

Fun Facts: Sweet potatoes are in fact not potatoes, which are tuber, but are swollen roots. Traditionally the water that sweet potatoes were boiled in was used to douse arthritic joints. Sweet potatoes, like many other substances, were used as a coffee substitute during the Civil War. Thin strips were dried out, ground and then brewed.

Super Food Facts: It's the red and purple skin of the sweet potatoes that is the true super food. These are packed full of vitamins A and C, two powerful antioxidants that are also beneficial for the skin, hair and nails. The cosmetic industry claims that they have anti-aging properties and have used them extensively in face care products. If these claims are true then why not just eat the vegetable? They also contain vitamins B2, B6, E and biotin and are high in magnesium and fibre. Sweet potatoes are great at facilitating digestion and regulating blood sugar levels and the presence of potassium and calcium helps ease and sooth stomach ulcers and other inflamed conditions. Sweet potatoes make an excellent weaning food for babies. An old, but popular sweet potato recipe is to boil them till soft, then mash with eggs and bake into a pie.

Gardening Tip: Sweet potatoes are prolific. They scramble through the garden with little regard for other plants. They like hot weather and given the right location, a patch of sweet potato can yield an enormous quantity. Make sure the soil has plenty of compost and good drainage. You can grow them from a cutting or you can simple bury a sweet potato, step back and watch it grow.

92. Tofu

Other Names: Firm tofu, soft tofu and silken tofu

Fun Facts: For hundreds of years tofu has been a staple food in Asian countries. It was a popular protein food for vegetarian Taoists.

Super Food Facts: Tofu is low in fat and sodium, contains no cholesterol and is high in vegetable protein making it ideal for vegetarians, vegans and people on a low-fat/cholesterol reducing diet. Tofu provides good amounts of B-vitamins and calcium, but it's the soy isoflavones that give it some interesting health benefits. Isoflavones are plant hormones that help reduce the symptoms of menopause, lower the rate of breast and prostate cancers and reduce the risk of osteoporosis.

Tofu, which is made from soybean curd, comes in different textures depending on its moisture content. Soft, silky tofu can be blended up with other ingredients to make cakes, pies, muffins and other baked goods. Firmer tofu is often cut into small chunks and mixed into stir-fries where it readily absorbs the other flavours.

Buying Tip: Tofu is available in most supermarkets and Asian stores. It is available in organic and flavoured varieties. Tofu should be covered with water and stored in the fridge in a plastic lidded container. Changing the water every second day will preserve and extend its shelf life.

93. Tomato

Other Names: *Lycopersicon esculentum*

Fun Facts: Kumatoes are a cross between a wild tomato from the Galapagos Islands and more conventional types. They are black/brown in colour and apparently more flavoursome and nutritionally dense than standard tomatoes. Some supermarket bought, flavourless tomatoes that have been picked green are mainly comprised of water and are not a super food.

Tomato

Super Food Facts: Vine ripened tomatoes are high in vitamins C and A. They are also rich in lycopene, which produces the red pigment. Lycopene has twice the antioxidant power of beta-carotene, which has been shown to inhibit prostate, colon, lung and stomach cancers.

Cooking tomatoes in olive oil helps release more of the lycopene and the oil helps the body absorb it. Tomato paste is an excellent alternative if no fresh produce is available. Most tomato paste products use vine-ripened tomatoes with a pinch of salt and oil. It's a concentrated form of lycopene and can be used as a bread-spread or on a pizza base.

Gardening Tip: There are many different varieties of tomatoes – some are easier to grow than others. For instance, cherry tomatoes grow like weeds in our vegetable gardens. Most tomatoes do well if they are staked as this keeps the fruit off the ground. They also grow best in a fertile, well-draining soil. Plant tomatoes in full-sun, mulch them well and water, water, water.

94. Tuna

Other Names: *Thunnus maccoyii* (Southern bluefin), *Thunnus thynnus* (Northern bluefin), albacore, slender tuna, yellowfin and frigate tuna

Fun Facts: In 2004 guidelines were issued warning pregnant women, nursing mothers and small children to limit their intake of larger species of tuna, such as bluefin and albacore because they are high in the food chain and possibly contaminated with mercury.

Super Food Facts: Tuna fish is an excellent source of protein, omega-3 fatty acids, potassium, selenium and vitamins D and B12. Tuna fish studies have demonstrated that it protects against Alzheimer's disease, high blood pressure, arthritis, deep vein thrombosis and that it can help reduce the risk of macular degeneration and dry eye syndrome. Some of the vitamin and mineral content of tuna is destroyed in the canning process, but canned tuna is still a very good source of protein and omega-3 fatty acids. Tuna can be eaten as a main dish, in salads, sandwiches, sashimi, dips and pastes.

Gardening Tip: Like most products of the sea (fish, shellfish and seaweed) Tuna frames make an excellent fertiliser (fish elusion) that can be diluted and watered into any garden bed or around fruit trees to condition the soil and increase crop size.

95. Turmeric

Other Names: *Curcuma domestica* and Indian saffron.

Fun Facts: Turmeric is a deep orange-yellow rhizomatous plant that is related to the ginger plant. Like ginger it packs a nutritional punch and both are popular in curries. Turmeric is also used as a dye.

Super Food Facts: Research into the active ingredient curcumin's medicinal properties has exploded over the last few years and much of this research points towards turmeric's antibacterial properties. Turmeric could also help prevent Alzheimer's disease and be a colorectal cancer inhibitor. Turmeric is often used with other spices to marinate meat before adding to a curry or stew. Its vibrant colour is evident in dishes such as chicken korma and vegetable pakora. It can also be mixed with water or pawpaw ointment and made into a paste that when rubbed into a wound inhibits bacterial infections.

Gardening Tip: Aside from the underground rhizomes, it is worth growing turmeric for its beautiful white flowers. Turmeric grows well in a hot, humid, monsoonal climate.

96. Wakame Seaweed

Other Names: *Undaria pinnatifid*

Fun Facts: According to the Global Invasion Species Database, wakame is among the top 100 invasive species, which is all the more reason to eat more of this super-sea vegetable.

Super Food Facts: Wakame is abundant in calcium, magnesium, manganese, folate, iron and vitamins A and C. However, it is also chock-full of sodium so people with high blood pressure and hypertension should avoid it. Wakame is like the lettuce of the sea. Use it fresh or rehydrate the dried wakame in soups, stews and wraps.

Gardening Tip: Wakame makes an excellent compost activator, garden fertiliser and soil improver. If you put wakame around plants, with some straw or lucerne on top, it acts like a slow release fertiliser and helps prevent water evaporation.

97. Watercress

Other Names: *Nasturtium officinale*

Fun Facts: There are over 40 medicinal uses for watercress including one listed by Pliny the Elder, stating that the smell could drive away snakes and poisonous insects. In more recent times it has been used a an all-round body cleanser because it is so high in chlorophyll.

Super Food Facts: Watercress is a slightly peppery, dark green leafy vegetable that sits right on top of the super food pyramid. It is very high in chlorophyll, folate, vitamins A, C and E and the minerals iron and calcium. Watercress is a member of the crucifer family and shares the same cancer-fighting properties as other members; kale, cauliflower, Brussels sprouts and cabbage. All lower the risk of colon and bladder cancers. Wash watercress thoroughly and avoid harvesting wild watercress as it can carry listeriosis.

Gardening Tip: Watercress can be grown in ponds or in a waterproof container. Large-scale watercress is grown in flooded fields like rice.

98. Wheatgerm ❶ ✸ ♥ 🌙 ☺

Other Names: *Triticum aestivum* and common wheat

Description: Humans have been eating wheat for more than 12,000 years and many cultures incorporated wheat into their seasonal rituals. Some cultures even have wheat gods and goddesses.

Super Food Facts: Wheatgerm and whole wheat are high in vitamin E and are a good source of B vitamins (folate, niacin, thiamine and B6), calcium, iron, protein, selenium, omega-3 fatty acids, zinc, manganese and magnesium. Wheat germ also contains octacosanol, which studies have shown increases endurance by improving the body's ability to provide oxygen to muscles and organ tissues. Adding wheatgerm to the diet can be as simple as sprinkling it on cereal, adding it to muffins, pizza bases, dips and casseroles. Store it in an airtight container in the fridge to prevent it going rancid.

Gardening Tip: Sprinkle wheat grass seeds all over the soil and rake in. Water regularly and when the wheat is all dried out harvest by cutting the heads off and leaving the stems. These can be used as mulch for the next crop.

99. Wheatgrass ✖ ✸ ♥ 🌙

Other Names: *Triticum aestivum*

Fun Facts: During the 1940s many studies into the medicinal benefits of liquid chlorophyll (wheatgrass juice) were conducted. It was discovered that wheatgrass, when young, is a high-density nutritional drink. Researchers also discovered that it wasn't just wheatgrass that had this high concentration of nutrients; many grasses showed similarly high levels and make an excellent nutritional supplement.

Super Food Facts: Wheatgrass juice is an extremely nutritionally dense drink and this is why it is taken as a small shot. It's all that's needed! Wheatgrass is high in chlorophyll, amino acids, mineral, vitamins and even enzymes. Two of the most apparent benefits of wheatgrass juice is an increase in energy levels and clear skin. The benefits of wheatgrass juice are obtained when it is raw, unprocessed, fresh and organic, but it can also be taken as a tablet or powder.

Gardening Tips: Wheatgrass is easy to grow. Use a tray and spread a little under a cup of wheatgrass seeds over the soil. Cover lightly with some more soil and keep moist.

100. Wild Rosella

Other Names: *Hibiscus sabdariffa* and red sorrel

Fun Facts: Wild Rosella naturalised in parts of Australia a few thousand years ago. There are other native varieties but the wild rosella flowers are the most commonly used. Aboriginals have eaten the roots and leaves of this plant.

Super Food Facts: The flowers of the wild rosella are bright red and are an incredibly rich source of vitamin C and antioxidants. Studies have shown it to have strong antihypertension properties and the flowers can be used in the treatment of liver diseases, respiratory illnesses and fever. The oil from the seeds is also a nutritional powerhouse that inhibits bacterial and fungal infections. Wild Rosella is most commonly made into jams and spreads and is used throughout the world in hot and cold drinks. It's particularly nice in a glass of champagne. Place the flower in the glass and fill with champagne.

Gardening Tip: Being a warm climate loving plant, wild rosellas love to be mulched with old compost, get plenty of sunlight and be protected from frosts.

Wild Rosella

101. Yoghurt

Other Names: Natural yoghurt and curd

Fun Facts: Yoghurt has two main super food properties. One is that it is an excellent source of calcium and the other is that it contains a bacteria that helps maintain intestinal integrity. It is particularly good for people with skin problems such as acne and can be used both internally and externally.

Super Food Facts: Good gut health is essential to absorb the nutrients from other super food sources. The best food to restore and maintain a healthy gut is plain, cultured yoghurt. It is one of the most important foods you can eat. The key to its remarkable health benefits lies in the live cultures that are added to the milk or cream. Live culture prevents the growth of harmful bacteria and yeast imbalances in the gut. Yoghurt is also a great source of calcium and protein. Yoghurt makers are cheap, economical and very easy to use. A single tablespoon of plain yoghurt mixed into hot (but not boiling milk) makes 1kg of natural yoghurt.

Buying Tip: Yoghurt has been used for thousands of years but it was only in the 1900s that it became commercialised and processed so that most yoghurts sold today are sweetened and not super foods. Plain cultured yoghurt, that tastes sour, is one of the best foods for maintaining an all over healthy immune system.

About the Author

Amber Mackenzie has an Advanced Certificate in Nutritional Science and has also written 'The Natural Pharmacy in Your Garden' in which her focus is growing and utilising health giving plants from your own garden. She lives in Bellingen NSW with her husband Josh and their two children Rosie and Elroy. Together they are building a house using new and recycled materials, vegetable and herb gardens and planted native and European fruit trees.

About the Illustrator

Liz Craig paints flora & fauna on paper, canvas, ceramic & silk, with the desire to convey the intricate beauty of the natural world to the wider community. She is based with her family on the NSW South Coast.

Disclaimer
This book contains descriptions and uses of medicinal and culinary plants of a general nature and should not be used in place of medical advice. Please see you doctor for a personalised, medical consultation.

Reference List

Allardice, Pamela, & Bone, Kerry, & Hutchinson, Frances. (1994). *Magic and Medicine of Plants*. Australia: Reader's Digest

Australian Macadamia Society. (2009). *Australian Macadamias: The Healthy Nut*. Retrieved November 27, 2009, from http://www.macadamias.org/pages/health-benefits

Australian Native Foods. (2008). *Plant profile: Bush tomato*. Retrieved December 3, 2009, from http://www.cse.csiro.au/research/nativefoods/crops/bushtomatoes.htm

Burnley, Lucy. (2004). *Superfoods for healthy kids: How to keeps your child's immune system fighting fit*. London: Duncan Baird Publishers.

Bush Tucker Shop: Kurrajong Australian Native Foods. (N.D.). *Whole bush tomato*. Retrieved December 3, 2009, from http://www.bushtuckershop.com/prod49.htm

Cherikoff, Vic. & Kowalski, George. (2009) *Super Foods for Super Health: Discover the wonders of Australian Native Fruits*. Sydney: Orielton Laboratories Pty.Ltd.

Daley's Fruit Tree Nursery. (2009). *Acai palm: Euterpa oleracea*. Retrieved December 3, 2009, from http://www.daleysfruit.com.au/Acai-Palm-Euterpe-Oleracea.htm

Delaterre, Flora. (N.D.). *Bitter Melon*. Flora Delaterre: The plant detective. Retrieved December 9, 2009, from http://www.floradelaterre.com/?id=38

Encyclopaedia Britannica. (2009). *Alfalfa: Main*. Retrieved December 3, 2009, from http://www.britannica.com/EBchecked/topic/14595/alfalfa

Flax and Linen. (2005). *Natural fibres*. Retrieved December 29, 2009, from http://www.binhaitimes.com/flax.html

Freedan, Louise. (2000). Wild About Mushrooms. Retrieved January 22, 2010, from http://www.mssf.org/cookbook/shiitake.html

Grieve, Mrs. M. (1931). *A Modern Herbal*. Retrieved November 26, 2009, from http://www.botanical.com/botanical/mgmh/a/apple044.html

HomeRemediesWeb. (N.D.). *Health Benefits of Alfalfa*. Retrieved December 3, 2009, from http://www.homeremediesweb.com/alfalfa_health_benefits.php

Kakadu International. (2008). *Australia's best Kept Secret*. Retrieved December 1, 2009, from http://www.kakadusuperjuice.com/

Keville, Kathy. (1994). *The Illustrated Herb Encyclopedia*. Sydney: Simon & Schuster.

Landon, Shane. (2008). *Highest Antioxidant content – Apple Report*. One a Day Super Food. Retrieved November 26, 2009, from www.oneadaysuperfood.com.au/pdfs/Apple_report.pdf

Low, Tim. (1999). *Australian Nature Feildguide: Wild Food Plants of Australia*. Australia: Harpercollins.

Lupu, Alexandra. (2006). *Exhaustive study to show multiple benefits of cranberries*. Softpedia: Health. Retrieved December 17, 2009, from http://news.softpedia.com/news/Exhaustive-Study-to-Show-Multiple-Benefits-of-Cranberries-40562.shtml

Mabey, David. (1978). In Search of Food: *Traditional Eating and Drinking in Britain*. Great Britain: Macdonald and Jane's Publishing.

Matelijan, George. (2009) *Brussels sprouts*. The World's Healthiest Foods. Retrieved December 10, 2009, from http://www.whfoods.com/newbook/bookannounce.html

Magicberry: The berry from the Gods. (N.D.). *The benefits of the Acai Berry explained*. Retrieved December 3, 2009, from http://www.magicberry.com.au/

Mori, Akio. (2006). *Capsaicin, a component of red peppers, inhibits the growth of androgen-independent, p53 mutant prostate cancer cells*. Cancer Research. Retrieved December 15, 2009, from http://cancerres.aacrjournals.org/cgi/content/abstract/66/6/3222

Mortenson, Jace. (N.D.). *Brussels sprouts get no respect*. Retrieved December 10, 2009, from http://www.drweil.com/drw/u/ART02025/brussels-sprouts.html

Ody, Penelope. (1993). *The complete medical herbal*. Victoria: Dorling Kindersley Limited.

Reader's Digest. (1997). *Foods that harm, foods that heal*. Surry Hills: Reader's Digest.

Rolfes, Sharon Rady, Pinna, Kathryn, & Whitney, Ellie. (2006). *Understanding normal and clinical nutrition* (7th ed.). Victoria: Thomson Learning Australia.

Sacks, FM. (2006). *Soy protein, isoflavones, and cardiovascular health: an American Heart Association Science Advisory for professionals from the Nutrition Committee.* PubMed.gov. Retrieved December 2, 2009, from http://www.ncbi.nlm.nih.gov/pubmed/16418439

Salt Spring Seeds. (2009). *Growing amaranth and quinoa (Dan's scoop).* Retrieved December 4, 2009, from http://www.saltspringseeds.com/scoop/powerfood.htm

Sexton, Mike. (2007). *Bush tucker may join list of 'super foods'.* Australian Bushfoods Magazine. Retrieved December 10, 2009, from http://www.ausbushfoods.com/index.php?option=com_content&task=view&id=101&Itemid=53

Stibich, Mark Ph.D. (N.D.). *The real story on the health properties of bee pollen.* About.com. Retrieved December 7, 2009, from http://longevity.about.com/od/antiagingfoods/a/bee_pollen.htm

Woods, Brian. (1995). Kakadu Plum. *The Australian New Crops Newsletter.* Retrieved December 1, 2009, from http://www.newcrops.uq.edu.au/newslett/ncnl4146.htm

Ye, Jiming. (2008). *A tonne of bitter melon produces sweet results for diabetes.* Garvan Institute: Breakthrough medical research. Retrieved December 8, 2009, from http://www.garvan.org.au/news-events/news/a-tonne-of-bitter-melon-produces-sweet-results-for-diabetes.html